p. 86

not enough about Elizabeth

as a person

*No. 4*
*Brief Lives*
QUEEN ELIZABETH

*Brief Lives*

# QUEEN ELIZABETH

*By*

*MILTON WALDMAN*

*BRIEF LIVES*
*COLLINS, ST JAMES'S PLACE*
*LONDON*

FIRST IMPRESSION      MARCH, 1952
SECOND IMPRESSION      OCTOBER, 1952

PRINTED IN GREAT BRITAIN
COLLINS CLEAR-TYPE PRESS : LONDON AND GLASGOW

*To*

PROFESSOR J. E. NEALE

*Master Elizabethan Mariner*

# CONTENTS

## * 1 *

## *Birth to Accession*

---

To the King of England and his new Queen it was beyond words important that the child they were expecting should be a boy: to the King, Henry VIII, because a son seemed essential to the preservation of the dynasty and even of England as an independent kingdom; to the Queen, Anne Boleyn, because she was highly unpopular and her chances of remaining Queen, indeed of remaining alive, might well depend on the child's being of the right sex. She had already seen, in his treatment of his former Queen, what the King was capable of doing to a wife who failed to provide him with the male heir he craved: even though that former Queen had been the Princess of a ruling house and not, like herself, a subject and a comparative upstart.

Henry was now forty-two and had been King since he was eighteen. In the first year of his reign he had married the Spanish Princess Catherine of

Aragon, the widow of his elder brother Arthur. They had had a number of children, but all of them had died almost immediately except one girl named Mary, now aged seventeen. For years this situation had deeply worried Henry, since the prospect of a woman on the throne after him seemed about the worst of imaginable disasters. The dynasty was still new and insecurely established: only six years before his birth his father, a Welsh adventurer by the name of Henry Tudor, had won the Crown from Richard III, the last of the Plantagenets, on the field of battle and assumed the title of Henry VII. Many, particularly amongst the older nobility, doubted and were prepared to dispute his right to it. Almost unceasing war between the great powers of the Continent made the time one of constant upheaval and danger. Only a man, it was universally agreed, would be able to deal with such dangers as these, and as the years went on Henry began to wonder whether his failure to have a son might not be a sign that Heaven was displeased with him about something. The only thing he could think of was a passage in the Old Testament which appeared to forbid marriage with a dead brother's wife. True, he had secured a dispensation from the Pope permitting him to marry Catherine, but after a while he began to wonder whether the Pope had the right to give such a dispensation; if not, he and

Catherine had never been lawfully married and were living in sin.

This worry became much more serious after he met and fell in love with Anne Boleyn, a sprightly, bright-eyed young lady who had returned from a long period at the Court of France to enter the service of Queen Catherine. For if he was not really married to Catherine, then he was free to marry Anne and have the sons Catherine had failed to give him. He put the question to the reigning Pope, Clement VII, who, after a good deal of hesitation, answered no: Henry was properly married and must stay so. Henry tried everything to make him change his mind—arguments, threats, and presently, with the aid of Parliament, a series of Acts drastically curtailing the Pope's powers and revenues in England. But the Pope stood firm, supported by Catherine's nephew Charles, the King of Spain, as well as by the majority of the English people, who, as Catholics of a thousand years' standing, began to be frightened by what they considered Henry's impieties. Nevertheless he went on, obtained from Parliament and a majority of the Bishops in Convocation the title of Supreme Head of the Church, thus ending England's allegiance to the Holy See, married Anne and a little while later had his marriage with Catherine pronounced null and void by the Archbishop of Canterbury, Thomas Cranmer. It was a

terrible risk, involving the peril of rebellion at home
and war abroad. Only one thing could have justified
it, Henry himself would probably have admitted, the
son for whose sake it had been incurred. So that
when the child, born at the riverside palace of
Greenwich on the Sunday afternoon of September
7th, 1533, turned out to be a girl, there really
seemed no point or purpose in its having been born
at all.

Nevertheless she was, for the time being, the sole
heiress to the throne—Mary having been dis-
possessed of that place as the result of Cranmer's
pronouncement—and welcomed as such with bells
ringing in the steeples and bonfires blazing in the
streets. Three days later, amidst pageantry of the
most magnificent splendour, she was christened at
the Church of the Grey Friars, adjacent to Greenwich
Palace, and given the name of Elizabeth after the
King's grandmother, Elizabeth of York. Some
seventy-five years later the poet who was to be the
chief glory of her reign made this ceremony the
concluding scene of his play *King Henry VIII* and had
her godfather, the Archbishop of Canterbury,
prophesy that

" *This royal infant . . .*
    *Though in her cradle, yet now promises*
    *Upon this land a thousand thousand blessings,*

*Which time shall bring to ripeness: she shall be,—*
*But few now living can behold that goodness,—*
*A pattern to all princes living with her,*
*And all that shall succeed: . . .*
*She shall be loved and feared: her own shall bless her;*
*Her foes shake like a field of beaten corn,*
*And hang their heads with sorrow . . .*

But Shakespeare was writing looking backwards. None of the great personages gathered round the royal infant's baptismal font would have bet a farthing that she would ever be Queen at all, let alone a famous and successful one. At best they expected her to marry a foreign Prince when she was old enough, one chosen by her father if he were still alive, in order to gain a useful ally, or, if he were dead, by the younger brother who would by then have come along to inherit the kingdom.

At the age of three months she was given a separate household, with a Governess, Margaret Lady Bryan, who had similarly brought up Mary, to look after her health and early training, and a staff of experienced officials to administer the household's various departments—accounts, furnishings, wardrobe, kitchens, stables, etc. This little Court did not long remain in one place but moved about, now to Hatfield, now to Hunsdon, now to the Bishop of Winchester's pleasant riverside manor at Chelsea.

The reason for these frequent moves was that large houses with many occupants tended in those days, because of their primitive sanitary arrangements, to become pestiferous after a while and had therefore to be vacated until they could be made, in the current phrase, ' sweet ' again. To London itself Elizabeth was seldom brought, visiting her parents either at Greenwich, which was as far from the town in one direction as Chelsea was in the other, or being visited by them, when they could spare the time, at her various country residences.

There was nothing unusual in this, nor any lack of love on her parents' part. It was merely considered best for children to be brought up away from the hubbub of the town and the Court, on which all the great business of State centred, by people skilled in and able to bring their whole minds to the task. The result was not, to judge by a letter of Lady Bryan's, as perfect as might have been hoped. Writing to the King's Chief Minister, Thomas Cromwell, she called his attention to the fact that the little Princess was practically destitute of clothing, under and outer, and of the materials to make them with; evidently it was as difficult for a royal governess to extract from the Treasury the necessary dresses and petticoats for a growing child as for the King's admirals and generals to persuade it to replace the guns and ammunition his forces

QUEEN ELIZABETH

*By an unknown artist*

were constantly using up. And, like the admirals and generals, the Governess found reason to complain that the correct performance of her duties was being improperly interfered with. Others in authority in the household insisted on spoiling the small Princess as soon as she was able to sit up to table by having her eat in public, where she saw and demanded things not good for her. " Alas, my Lord, it is not meet for a child to keep such rule yet. I promise you, my Lord, I dare not take it upon me to keep her Grace in health and she keep that rule; for there shall she see divers meats and fruits and wine, which would be hard for me to refrain her Grace from. Ye know, my Lord, there is no place of correction there. And she is yet too young to correct greatly."

However sensibly and carefully they might be brought up, there was always danger of a king's children being spoilt, since all royal persons tended to be thought of and treated as a kind of higher species than ordinary mortals. There was, however, one limit to this danger: if the King himself frowned on any one, even of his own family, every one else was likely to follow suit. An example of this occurred in Elizabeth's household shortly after it was established at Hatfield. Her half-sister Mary was in disgrace for having refused to recognise her father as Supreme Head of the Church or to accept Anne as his wife and Queen in place of her own mother. Anne was naturally furious and persuaded Henry to punish Mary for her disobedience by putting her in the control of Anne's friends and followers at Hatfield. There she was not only treated as her baby sister's inferior and dependent, but insulted, kept virtually imprisoned and threatened with beatings if she would not yield. Though she suffered, in pride even more than body, she remained firm, but her sufferings could not but affect her feelings towards Elizabeth, their innocent cause. The effect was to be important in the lives of both the sisters.

Then, quite suddenly, when Elizabeth was two and a half, the situation took a dramatic turn. Henry had already fallen out of love with Anne and in love with somebody else. A second divorce would have been dangerous, for with Anne out of the way the people might have considered that he was still married to Catherine, who was as widely beloved as Anne was hated; moreover, Anne was expecting a baby who might turn out to be the long-awaited heir. But in January, 1536, Catherine died and when Anne's baby, a boy, was born shortly afterwards, it was found to be already dead. The King felt mocked and disappointed as he had been with Catherine; and not having the same respect for Anne, he took a shorter and more dreadful way to be rid of her. She was accused of having had other lovers than himself, which by law was high treason, and after a hasty and dishonest trial was beheaded on Tower Hill. Her marriage with Henry was pronounced null and void in the same way that Catherine's had been, and Elizabeth, like Mary, thus declared illegitimate and disqualified from succeeding to the throne. At the same time Henry took the other lady, Jane Seymour, for his third wife.

Of these tremendous events and what they signified for herself Elizabeth of course remained ignorant until she was older. She was not a problem like Mary, now twenty, and Henry felt and acted towards her exactly as before. Mary still had a period of suffering to go through, because after his third marriage Henry insisted that she must once and for all approve of what he had done, and had her secluded and ill-treated until she signed a paper acknowledging her own illegitimacy and her father's supremacy over the English Church. Restored to favour, she once more joined Elizabeth's household, but this time as an equal, and for the next few years the two sisters, though only occasionally under the same roof, developed a fondness for each other which lasted until as grown women they came into inevitable conflict. But for the present there was no cause of rivalry and still less after Henry's new wife presented him with a son in October, 1537, thus settling the long-vexed question of the succession to

Q.E.                                                    B

the general satisfaction. At his baptism, where he received the name Edward after his great-great-grandfather, Edward IV, Mary acted as his god-mother and Elizabeth carried the christening robe, or rather—because she was still too small at four to stand up through the long ceremony—she carried the heavily-jewelled robe while two stout peers of the realm carried her.

The change in her position in no way diminished the care and thought given to her education. She was still the King's daughter, after all, and even if ineligible for the throne, more important than any one else's daughter; and daughters were considered, at least amongst the upper classes, entitled to have as much care given to their education as sons. The educational standards of the Renaissance were high and stern. By the time she was six Elizabeth, like Mary before her and Edward after her, would have been reading Latin as well as English, at ten writing and speaking it fluently. By then we know from her teachers that she had already begun French and Italian, and soon added Greek, which she was to continue even after she was Queen. At the same time she was receiving her religious instruction, which was so intimately related to the classical that in her early 'teens she was " doing " the Greek Testament and the Latin Fathers of the Church, like Saints Jerome and Augustine, in the original as well as the great pagan writers like Sophocles, Demosthenes, Cicero and Livy.

At this stage she would also have begun exploring the sciences, particularly arithmetic, elementary physics and astronomy, in which the startling discoveries of Copernicus about the heavens were just being made known to the world by his followers. With these would have been included in the course of time such formal and methodical studies as logic and rhetoric to help her arrange her thoughts and utter them with clarity and precision. Music too, although one of the earliest of her studies, in a sense belonged to this category, for though an art loved and practised by everybody, it was also a science with its rules and theories which any serious student had to master before venturing upon composition; to compose music well was almost as necessary for a cultivated person as to play and sing it well. Elizabeth, like Mary, was a more than ordinarily good performer on the virginals and the lute, but neither ever came near to their father as a composer, for some of his works give delight to the present day. Then there was sport, not a mere pastime but an activity with its own strict discipline in which every boy and girl not an outright invalid was expected to excel, and in which Elizabeth, both as horsewoman and archer, did excel, though again not so greatly as her father, one of the best athletes in all Europe.

All this left but little time for the purely feminine accomplishments such as the different kinds of needlework, which had also to be mastered and put to use in making Christmas, or rather New Year, and birthday presents for her relatives and friends.

It was a heavy programme for young people and perhaps helps to explain why, in practically all the portraits we have of children of the Tudor period, they wear the same grave, pre-occupied expressions as their elders, just as from earliest infancy they wear the same kind of clothes, full of jewels and furs and feathers and fuss. When religious devotions, sleeping and eating are taken into account, there seems to be little if any time allowed for spontaneous play. There were, of course, the various seasonal festivities at Christmas, Twelfth Night, etc., with their appropriate fun and games, plays and dancing, but these were in general as well organised as the studies. It was not so much in those special occasions that the young folk were expected to find relief and recreation as in the studies themselves, in the change from one thing to another, the balance of one against another, that made the whole easier to carry. In this an effort was made to approach the classical ideal of *mens sana in corpore sano*—a sound mind in a sound body—which had been adopted and was preached by so many famous scholars of the time, including the Spaniard Vives and the Englishman

Ascham, who laid down the general lines of Mary's and Elizabeth's education respectively.

In this way the years passed, uneventfully despite the tremendous events going on in the world outside, and not unhappily despite the absence of the family life which is the usual centre of a child's existence. Her mother she could not remember, her father as always was a remote and splendid figure whose habit of turning up so frequently with a different wife must have been somewhat bewildering: for Queen Jane died when Edward was born, and presently there was the pleasant German lady, Anne of Cleves, whom Henry quickly divorced, and soon afterwards Catherine Howard whom, like Anne Boleyn, he caused to be executed, and finally Catherine Parr, who survived him. Such family affection as she had went out chiefly to her little brother, the nearest to her in age, and some of her most joyous times were her reunions with him, sometimes at his house or hers, sometimes with their father and sister also present at St. James's or Whitehall Palace for the great seasonal festivities. But ordinarily she lived with governesses and guardians, who as she grew older increasingly lost authority over her and deferred to her as mistress of her own household. So that when Henry VIII died, five months after Elizabeth's thirteenth birthday, she was not so unready as a less precocious child in a less precocious age would be to confront the dangers and responsibilities of her rank and blood.

The dangers lay in the fact that her rank and blood once more corresponded to each other. By his will, enacted into law by Parliament two years before his death, Henry had provided that if Edward died childless he was to be succeeded by Mary, and she, if she also died childless, by Elizabeth. So Elizabeth resumed her natural and proper place in the order of succession, and thereby at once became a person of the most tremendous consequence. For it seemed quite likely that Edward, a sickly little boy of nine, would not grow to manhood, and that Mary, a frail, tiny, pink-and-white spinster of thirty-one, might, even if she survived him, not be allowed, despite her father's will, to succeed to the throne; for, as a staunch Catholic, many who believed in or had grown rich out of the Reformation would be opposed to her, lest she restore the Catholic faith and compel those who had profited out of the pillage of the Church to restore their gains. Thus the eyes of many were fixed on Elizabeth, not as a barely possible Queen in a problematical future, but as a quite probable one when certain things happened. And that of course rendered her situation dangerous because others' eyes rested watchfully upon her to

see that ambition and discontent did not use her for
their own unlawful purposes.

Nevertheless they did, once in her brother's reign
and once in her sister's. After her father's death she
went to live for a while with his widow, Catherine
Parr. Stepmother and stepdaughter were fond of
each other; both had been brought up in the
Protestant way of thinking that had begun to
prevail at Court towards the end of Henry VIII's
life, and each admired the other's mind and character. Some of Elizabeth's earliest literary efforts, a
translation from the French and a religious medita-
tion, were inspired by the wish to please Catherine,
and some of the most careful work of her needle
were meant as gifts for her. But this pleasant
relationship was presently disturbed by a man—an
unusually good-looking, finely-built man in his
thirties, Thomas Seymour, Lord High Admiral of
England, with whom Catherine had been more than
half in love before Henry married her: the King's
proposal had, of course, amounted to a command
and could not be refused. Now she was free, but
Seymour at first thought of looking higher. Under
Henry's will sixteen Regents were named to govern
the Kingdom until Edward VI came of age. This
provision the Regents themselves almost immediately
altered by electing one of their number, Viscount
Hertford, the young King's uncle, to head the

government under the title of Protector. Now Hertford, otherwise Edward Seymour, was Thomas's elder brother—both being brothers of the late Queen Jane—and Thomas was exceedingly jealous of his elevation, deeming himself the better man and, by virtue of being equally the King's uncle, equally entitled to the highest place under him. As a matter of fact he had gained as the result of his brother's elevation, having been made a baron and a Privy Councillor as well as Lord Admiral, but this altogether failed to satisfy his conceit, especially when Hertford was created Duke of Somerset as well as Protector. In the hope of improving his position he sought to marry one of the King's sisters, but made no progress with either, the thirteen-and-a-half-year-old Elizabeth informing him that " even when she shall have reached years of discretion " she had no intention of marrying—a truer statement than perhaps even she at the time suspected. Seymour then fell back on his former sweetheart, Catherine Parr, and married her within what was felt to be a shockingly short time, three months or less after Henry's death.

But more shocking things were to follow. Elizabeth continued to live with the newly-married couple at their house by the river in Chelsea; and Seymour continued to pay attention to her far beyond what was proper from a married man to a young girl.

Some of the attentions he paid to her—such as coming to her bedroom to wake her in the morning by drawing the curtains of her four-poster bed and then tickling or smacking her—seemed most improper, but since his wife apparently knew about it and did not disapprove, nothing much could be said. But later Catherine herself apparently began to feel uneasy and jealous, and presently, when she was expecting a baby, asked Elizabeth to go. They parted on friendly terms, however, and continued to correspond after Elizabeth had set up her own house again in Hertfordshire.

On September 7th, 1548, Elizabeth's fifteenth birthday, Catherine died giving birth to her baby. Throughout their brief marriage Seymour had been scheming and working towards the day when he might turn out and replace his brother. He had made friends with his nephew the King by giving him presents of money and contrasting his own generosity with the stinginess of the Protector; he had tried to assert control of the King's person and, failing that, to have him declared of age so that the Protectorship would automatically end; and meantime he had been building up a party and corrupting various royal officials by bribes and flattery. So far he had accomplished nothing by it all except to draw on himself the suspicions of the Protector and his government. But with his wife's death the prospect suddenly changed. He was once more free to offer himself to Elizabeth and this time, he fancied, with a better chance of success. Once he had made himself her husband, no rival but would have to look up to the King's brother-in-law, who, as Consort to his quite probable heiress, would one day share the throne with her.

So far as Elizabeth was concerned, he was not far wrong about her feelings. His manly good looks and gay good humour had left their impression; the memory of his attentions still had the power to bring the warm blushes to her pale olive cheeks; and there were those about her to see to it that he and the emotions he aroused did not quickly fade from her imagination. Her governess, Mrs. Ashley, had been quite as smitten with the Admiral as the girl herself. With evident regret she mentioned to Elizabeth that it had been she and not Catherine whom he had wanted to marry, and declared that it was what Henry VIII had wanted too; and she and Elizabeth would tell fortunes with cards in which " Seymour " would frequently emerge from the pack amidst much giggling and joking. But more serious than all this were the journeys of Thomas Parry, the Household treasurer, or Cofferer, to town for long serious conferences with Seymour. By her father's will Elizabeth had been left lands yielding an income of roughly £3,500 a year. Seymour wanted her to press

for the grant of the letters patent which would place
her in control of this money, and also to insist that
the lands should be in the West Country, touching
his own, so that their two lots of tenants could be
treated as one in case the need arose to use them
as a military force. All this had to be done very
quietly, for if the government learned of it, not only
would the grant of the lands be put off but every
precaution taken to prevent the marriage. So
Seymour talked to Parry and Parry came home to
talk to Mrs. Ashley, who gave him the most reassur-
ing messages to take back to the Admiral. But in
fact she did this on her own authority, for Elizabeth
at fifteen was already too prudent to commit herself
to courses she did not understand and had no hope
of controlling.

The government were not fooled, however. The
Protector and his advisers had all along had their
eyes on Seymour's activities, including his approaches
to Elizabeth. When they felt that he had gone far
enough, that he was on the verge of doing something
irretrievable out of which an insurrection might
spring, they ordered his arrest and sent him to the
Tower on a charge of high treason. Four days later,
on January 21st, 1549, Mrs. Ashley and Parry were
also removed to the Tower, to be closely questioned
as to what they, Seymour and Elizabeth had been
up to, and Sir Robert Tyrwhitt, a member of the

Privy Council, at the same time sent to Hatfield to examine Elizabeth herself. It was a tense and delicate moment for her. She could not possibly know what Seymour had said nor what Mrs. Ashley or Parry might say; she might be implicated in deeds she had never heard of or confessions she had not made. In fact that is what nearly happened. For a week none of the three in the Tower nor the girl at Hatfield would speak—then Parry, goaded by a false report of something Mrs. Ashley had said against him, turned on her and told all that she had told him on the topic of Seymour and Elizabeth. Mrs. Ashley was then confronted with Parry's statement, and when she still refused to say anything, with Parry himself: against whom she then became so angry at his accusing her that she accused him; and pretty soon, under the clever questioning of the officials present, the whole story was out.

Then it was carried to Elizabeth. If she admitted it she confessed herself guilty of complicity in Seymour's treason; if she denied it nobody would believe her in face of the statements of her two most intimate servants. That she would be put to death was unlikely, being so young and the King's sister, but there was every danger, if she failed to clear herself, of being disqualified from the succession and kept in prison until she could be got rid of by marriage to some nonentity abroad. Moreover, she had not only herself to protect but the two servants whom she loved—loved them enough, indeed, to take them back into her confidence when she was Queen despite their having let her down. Unable to deny what they had said, particularly as their sworn statements were shown her in their own handwriting, she stoutly denied that those statements meant what they seemed to mean. Tyrwhitt tried again and again to penetrate to whatever secrets may have lain hidden behind her round childish face and innocent blue eyes, but all his remorseless questioning was in vain. She only reiterated, haughtily and even indignantly, that she had never done any plotting with Seymour; that Mrs. Ashley had never proposed such a thing to her, nor so far as she knew had Seymour ever proposed it to Mrs. Ashley. She may have been indiscreet, even immodest, but that was not the same thing as being criminal. Let them make what they could of that.

So far as she was concerned they could make nothing. They brought in a girl she liked, to draw more out of her; they placed Tyrwhitt's wife as a stern governess over her in place of Mrs. Ashley, to her angry and frightened displeasure. But nothing succeeded, nothing could succeed if she kept her wits cool under her flaming red hair and her quivering lips firmly pressed together against any unlucky slips. In the end the government had to let her off

and restore her servants to her, while Seymour went
to the block for the misdeeds with which they had
failed to connect her. On hearing of his death she
is reported to have said, with justice but astonishing
cold-bloodedness considering how fond she had been
of him, " This day died a man of much wit but very
little judgment." In this she was not altogether
singular, for the eleven-year-old Edward, who had
accepted many favours from him, expressed pretty
much the same feelings. These Tudor Princes were
and had to be a pretty cold-blooded lot to keep
alive at all.

Elizabeth's next ordeal was in fact to involve her
life, since not only was she older but the charge
against her was more serious and many powerful
people wanted her permanently out of the way. But
meanwhile she had five years of comparative peace
—years of study, mostly, some of them with the
famous Roger Ascham, in the quiet of Hatfield or
Cheshunt, varied by afternoons of sport and evenings
of music, and occasionally by visits to Court to see
her brother the King. The grave troubles of his
reign scarcely touched her, though they fell heavily
on Mary. Greater changes were made in the religion
of England by the Protector's government in those
few years than had occurred in the previous thousand,
Henry's included. Archbishop Cranmer's two Books

of Common Prayer replaced the old Catholic services and in many respects introduced innovations so radical that even later generations of Protestants would refuse to retain them. Elizabeth had no difficulty in conforming to these changes since she, like Edward, had been brought up largely by the Reformers. But Mary, a Catholic to her marrow, refused, as did many thousands of less important people. In the south-western and eastern counties there were armed rebellions which were fiercely put down, but Mary, though harassed and persecuted, continued to have Mass said daily in her private chapel.

It was she also who bore the brunt of the great troubles that followed on Edward's death and saved the Crown not only for herself but eventually for Elizabeth. Some years earlier the Protector had been replaced at the head of affairs by an able but un-scrupulous adventurer, John Dudley, Duke of Northumberland, who had imprisoned him and later had him executed. For nearly three years North-umberland remained supreme, making a great deal of money and a great many enemies, but safe so long as Edward lived. By the summer of 1553, however, it became obvious to every one that Edward was dying, and Northumberland saw that desperate measures were called for; mercy he could hardly expect, let alone high office, either from his numerous foes or from the heir to the throne, whom he had so persecuted because of her religion. He had a paper drawn up and presented it to the dying King for his signature, assuring him that it was the only possible way to save the Protestant faith in England. This paper set aside Henry VIII's will to the extent of removing Mary and Elizabeth from the succession and putting in their place their cousin Lady Jane Grey, whom Northumberland had already caused to be married to one of his own sons.

With Edward he had no difficulty, and the others whose consent he required he bullied and threatened until they gave in. Having the Army and Navy at his command all he now needed was the possession of Mary for his plan to succeed. But Mary, who had been on her way to visit her brother in his last illness, eluded Northumberland's cavalry and fled into East Anglia. With incredible speed the whole country rose on her behalf. Within a few days Northumberland, who had set out in pursuit of her, was obliged to recognise her as the rightful Queen. On this news Elizabeth left Hatfield for London with the largest and most brilliant band of armed retainers she could muster. After a short pause at Somerset House she set out again with her train to meet Mary and the two sisters rode into London together for Mary's wonderful reception from her people.

For a little while all went well. At the coronation Elizabeth rode with Anne of Cleves, her father's only surviving wife, directly behind Mary in the same sort of " red chariot covered with cloth of silver." But the friendliness could not last long. Soon Mary, as was to be expected, had restored the Mass in the royal chapel, and everybody knew that when Parliament met that autumn the religious laws of Edward VI would be repealed and the religion of England restored to what it had been at Henry's death: with the strong probability that in due course Henry's changes would also be wiped out and England revert to her ancient obedience to the Holy See. Many people would object to this, some because their consciences would be violated, others— chiefly amongst the rich and powerful—because the lands and goods of which the Church had been despoiled were now in their hands and they feared that a return to the old religion might require them to be restored to their original owners. Such people could not help wishing that there were someone else on the throne than an uncompromising Catholic like Mary; and neither they nor she could help remembering that there really was no one else to put in her place except Elizabeth. This alone would have made for bad feeling. But when Mary remembered what she and her mother had suffered on account of Elizabeth's mother; and when she recalled how lightly the younger girl took the whole question of religion—how easily she had made one profession of faith in her father's time and quite another in her brother's—it is easy to understand how the elder, to whom religion was the most important of all things, could not but be suspicious when Elizabeth now declared herself ready to become a Catholic and to take this readiness not as a proof of sincere belief but of a scheming and untrustworthy character.

Within six months of the two sisters entering London together Mary's suspicions had become a certainty. Almost her first act had been to go to the Tower and there release various prisoners of State. Most important of them was young Edward Courtenay, who had spent fifteen of his twenty-seven years in captivity following the execution of his father, the Marquess of Exeter, by Henry. For this reason he enjoyed a wide popular sympathy, as well as for his charm and good looks. He was of the most illustrious blood in England, a Plantagenet of the House of York, a great-grandson of Edward IV and therefore heir to the claims of the White Rose which Henry VII had usurped, as many thought, on Bosworth Field. All those who thought so, and a great many more, felt that Mary would be wise to marry him for a variety of reasons. A husband of some sort she must have, on that all were agreed, for a woman ruling alone was hardly imaginable;

apart from any question of ability, there was her duty to rear the children by whom the dynasty must be carried on. Were the husband to be a foreigner, argued Courtenay's supporters, there was danger of England coming under foreign domination: better to take the most eligible of Englishmen and thus strengthen the Tudors' somewhat doubtful, because very recent, claims to the throne, and in so doing finally heal the last scars left in people's memories by the Wars of the Roses.

The argument left Mary unimpressed. Though prepared to favour Courtenay because of his sufferings and his birth—she soon made him Earl of Devon—she would not marry him: partly because she saw that he was vain, unstable and immoral, partly because she had made up her mind to marry someone else. During the whole of her troubled life she had been accustomed to rely for help and advice on her cousin the King of Spain and Holy Roman Emperor, Charles V. He had a son Philip, of the same age as Courtenay. Charles very much wanted her to marry Philip in the hope that he would thus gain English support in the long struggle he was waging with France for the mastery of Europe. Mary felt drawn to the marriage, in the first instance by the desire to be more closely united to her friend and benefactor, but later, after receiving the gift of Philip's portrait, because she also found the neat, fair-haired little Prince with the sad blue eyes and prominent jaw much to her taste. A number of her ministers agreed that the marriage might be a good thing for England, a small and weak country by comparison with rich and mighty Spain. But the majority objected strongly, urging that the marriage would make of England a mere satellite of the larger country.

With this view most of the English people seemed to agree, in particular those who lived in and round London. When the Emperor's ambassadors came over in January, 1554, to sign the marriage treaty, the people glared at them with sullen hostility and the little boys in the streets flung hard-packed snow-balls at their grave faces and the gay waving plumes in their hats. By the end of the month hatred of the marriage had led to armed risings, the most serious of them in the region of London, towards which Sir Thomas Wyatt led a strong force from Kent. The common object of all the risings was to prevent Mary sharing her throne with the Spaniard by marrying Elizabeth to Courtenay and setting them in her place. Had not Mary by a great speech at the Guildhall aroused the Londoners in her favour the rebellion might well have succeeded. Wyatt led his force to the very gates of the City, expecting there to be welcomed by the populace amongst whom his chief support was supposed to be. But they, now stirred to enthusiasm for their Queen, refused to admit him and instead handed him and his followers over to her officers.

A few days before this Mary, aware that something serious was brewing, had written to Elizabeth, then living at Ashbridge, suggesting that she come to London. The object of the invitation was to get her out of harm's way before the rebels could make use of her for their purposes. Elizabeth took her time answering and finally wrote to say that she could not come just then because of ill-health. This in itself was suspicious: but meantime the government had discovered what appeared to be grave evidence against her, and Mary, immediately after Wyatt's defeat, sent several of her ministers and physicians accompanied by an armed force to bring her to London if they found that she was fit to be moved. Elizabeth pleaded hard, claiming that she was still unwell. The physicians admitted that she was—and indeed the strain she had of late been under would have told on anybody—but declared that she was well enough to travel. Elizabeth made the journey as slowly as possible, but eventually the cavalcade arrived and the Queen's examiners set to work. They knew already that France had given support to Wyatt, spurring him on with promises of arms and money. That anybody might have guessed, as the French would obviously do almost anything to prevent their great enemy Spain from gaining advantage in England through the marriage of its Prince with the English Queen. The examiners also knew that at the time Mary had invited Elizabeth to London, Wyatt had his plans for moving her farther away, out of the Queen's reach. The question was how much Elizabeth knew of all this: if it could be proved that she had encouraged Wyatt to deal with a foreign Power in order to put her on the throne, that would be high treason of the worst sort and the end of her. That was what many important people wanted, in England and out, chief of them the Emperor, for with Elizabeth's death the principal motive for conspiracies against Mary would be removed and Philip be able to come in safety to marry her. Indeed, so heartily did the high Catholic, pro-Spanish party desire this that they would have been ready to put Elizabeth to death as a public menace without any trial at all. Luckily for her the heiress to the Crown could not very well be done away with as inconvenient, like lesser folk, merely because some would have preferred it so.

To all the questions regarding her dealings with Wyatt she reiterated that she had not had any; and regarding his dealings with France, that she knew nothing about them. Then how, demanded the examiners, did she account for the letter they were

able to produce? It was a copy of her own letter
to Mary refusing to come to London, and had been
found in the French ambassador's post-bag, stolen
from his courier on its way to France by pretended
highwaymen in the employ of the English government. Elizabeth could not explain it, she could only
surmise that it had been taken by one of her servants
and given or sold to one of Wyatt's or the French
Ambassador's agents. The examiners were not
satisfied. They could not convict her on the
evidence, but equally they would not let her go. In
the end they decided to remand her to the Tower
for further investigation.

It must have been the most fearful day of her
long and eventful life, the dismal rainy Sunday in
March on which they carried her by barge from
Whitehall Stairs to the grim old prison on the
Thames. So many had gone in at that gate and
never come out—her own mother amongst them—
but been thrown headless into a grave in the little
church of St. Peter's within the Tower walls. No
wonder that on disembarkation at those fatal steps
her legs gave under her and she sank down upon the
wet stones. But her courage soon revived and without help she rose and walked in with head erect,
protesting her innocence and loyalty. Nor could her
inquisitors thereafter make her take back or alter
a syllable. That was as well, for had she lost her

head figuratively she would almost certainly have lost it literally.

Failing to get anything directly out of the prisoner, the Crown kept her in the Tower and Wyatt alive beyond the usual time in the hope of getting something more out of him. In that they failed, and when he went to the scaffold in April he died declaring her innocence. In May the government decided that it could neither with decency kill her nor keep her under close arrest, nor on the other hand safely let her go free for the present. So she was sent to Woodstock in Oxfordshire in charge of stern but honest old Sir Henry Bedingfield, who had performed the same office towards Queen Catherine twenty years before. Elizabeth was not Catherine, to submit with patience; she teased, she wheedled, she puzzled her strait-laced, well-meaning keeper till he did not know whether he was on his head or his heels, and while he was exhorting her to attend to her Cicero, she was inducing him to violate his orders by allowing her to communicate with her friends outside, and to put her case to the authorities, even the Queen, until she succeeded, by sheer persistence in making a nuisance of herself, in getting the orders changed. But whether she had really been guilty of plotting neither he nor any one else ever found out for certain. Elizabeth herself, obviously amused at her own cleverness—as she had every right to be—put the matter as well as it could be put in the cryptic little rhyme she scratched with a diamond on the window at Woodstock:

> *Much suspected by me,*
> *Nothing proved can be.*

When, after two years, Mary agreed to see her again at Court, where she tried to draw some sort of admission from her, Elizabeth with downcast eyes merely declared that, although innocent, it would be improper for her to contradict the Queen, and Mary ended with a sigh of " God knows," with which the matter had finally to rest.

Yet her escape, and the manner of it, was of inestimable consequence for Elizabeth. Mary married Philip at Winchester in July, after Elizabeth's release from the Tower, and for long hoped to have a baby who would settle the succession without further reference to Elizabeth. But she never had the baby, and meantime, owing to the burning of the Protestants and other causes not all of them her fault, poor Mary lost the love of her people along with her happiness and her health. Presently Philip, by then King of Spain, did in fact drag England into an unpopular war with France, as his enemies had always predicted he would—a war in which Spain with English help gained a spectacular victory and England, with the loss of Calais, sustained an even more spectacular defeat. This ended Mary's popularity, what remained of it, and virtually her life. Spain, which had only a few years earlier clamoured for Elizabeth to be killed, now came round to the idea of her succeeding her ailing and childless sister. Little as Mary liked the idea, she could suggest nothing better, nor would the English people, since Elizabeth's reputation had been cleared of stain, have accepted any other successor than the one appointed by nature and by law. Shortly after Mary's death in the raw early hours of November 17th, 1558, the two Houses of Parliament met and without a dissenting voice proclaimed Henry VIII's last surviving child, the twenty-five-year-old Elizabeth, their Queen.

# ★ 2 ★

## The New Queen

---

IN ALL her long reign Elizabeth never saw most of the land over which she ruled. Though a frequent traveller who nearly every year made what was called a Progress through part of her realm, she found it impossible to visit Devon, Cornwall, Wales, most of the Midlands or any of the North. The time and the difficulties would have been too great. On the occasion of visiting Bristol she gave thanks to the Almighty for having preserved her through so long a journey. For England was then still almost entirely rural, in many respects primitive, groups of farms and villages separated from one another by vast tracts of forest through and round which meandered a few roads so poor, and in the rainy season so impassable owing to the mud, that it was quicker, safer and cheaper for goods to be moved to the nearest port and thence by sea. Apart from London, with its 200,000 inhabitants, there was no city of over 30,000, little manufacturing except on a small scale, and, apart from Cornish tin and Northumbrian coal, practically no mining. Iron and steel were largely bought abroad and even that made at home was smelted by wood rather than coal. The exact population is not known but could not have much exceeded 3,500,000.

By far the greater number gained their living by farming, in which the rearing of sheep for wool played an increasingly important part. Wool was, indeed, the keystone of the national economy. It was the chief export, both raw and in the form of home-made cloths, the means by which England paid for most of her imported luxuries and kept much of her shipping occupied. It also largely determined her political relationships, which tended to friendship with Spain because Spain ruled the Low Countries, the principal buyer of her wool and woollen goods; it was the reason why the loss of Calais, her chief port of entry for wool' on the Continent, was regarded as so grave a disaster. But there was also another side to it. In most respects England was self-supporting; her " abundance of necessaries " was mentioned with envy and admiration by foreigners who considered her in other respects backward and under-developed; but the growing, if still comparatively small, industries, needed imports—dyes, for instance—and her rich had developed a keen appetite for luxuries—brocades, laces, tapestries, cloth-of-gold, rare foods and spices—which could only be obtained from abroad.

Such things had to be paid for in money. The product that earned the money was chiefly wool. So the rich and powerful had by one means and another sought to acquire ploughland in order to turn it into pasture for sheep. Much of this land had been tilled by its inhabitants in common from time immemorial to supply their own needs. The enclosure and conversion of this land to grazing turned thousands loose to gain their living in whatever way they might or with their families become public charges or starve. But even this could not satisfy the money-hunger of the new owners: for after the discovery of America about half a century before, great quantities of silver and gold began to pour into Europe and drove up the price of everything, according to the general rule which declares that the greater the quantity of money there is in proportion to goods, the higher the price of the goods. So still more land was enclosed and given over to sheep to meet the needs of the rich, who thus grew richer while the poor grew poorer. Not all, of course; there were many exceptions on both sides; but this was the tendency.

Amongst those who grew poorer was the Crown. Taxes were voted irregularly, and as a rule unwillingly, by Parliament, and collected inefficiently by the local officials in the counties; the bulk of the Crown's revenues, out of which it had to defray the expenses of the Court, the armed forces and such civil services as then existed, came from its lands, which were mostly let out on ancient leases and paid rents absurdly low by comparison with the fast-rising costs of the time. Henry VIII had tried to make up the deficit by debasing the currency, that is, mixing English coins with base metal in place of the full amount of gold or silver they were supposed to contain, and pocketing the difference. But sellers, knowing this, raised the price of their wares in the same proportion, with the result that English merchants buying abroad had to pay higher prices in terms of their own money, and sell dearer at home. It was a system of inflation not dissimilar to that which we have seen in our time, though we now deal in cheques and paper rather than gold and silver, and had similar results in disturbing the even relationship between costs and prices so important to people who have to gain their daily living.

This was only one of the problems that confronted Elizabeth at her accession. There were others even more pressing if the kingdom were to be safe and prosper. Internally it was divided by deep dissensions amongst its people, externally it was weak by comparison with its nearest continental neighbours. Within less than twenty years it had been forcibly subjected to three different kinds of religion, a sort of Anglo-Catholicism under Henry VIII, an extreme Protestantism under Edward and the old orthodox Catholicism under Mary. Such a thing as toleration, each person worshipping according to his own conscience, was inconceivable; all had to worship the same way, and each change had been accompanied by persecution and left a legacy of hatred amongst those who preferred another way. Whatever course the new Queen adopted she would make enemies, while to adopt none would be the worst course of all, since that would leave it to the various creeds to fight it out amongst themselves until one had crushed the rest. Apart from these religious quarrels there were sectional differences. The West, including Wales and the North, had different ways of life and thought from those parts nearer the capital, and did not want to be interfered with; while in Ireland, English domination over a hostile race could only be maintained by a constant expenditure of lives, money and watchfulness.

Alongside and closely related to these perils threatening the country from within were the perils threatening it from without. France and Spain, the two great Powers long locked in a struggle for the mastery of the Continent, could tolerate no neutrals: at least none like England, which, because of her position, could close the vital passage through the

Channel and the North Sea to either by becoming the ally of the other. Either, on the other hand, might endanger and perhaps entirely stop England's trade with the Continent through those waters; France had already done it grave damage and might jeopardise it further by her recent seizure of Calais. Moreover, France virtually controlled Scotland, where the mother of the young Queen ruled as Regent for her daughter, lately married to the Dauphin in Paris, and where French troops lay encamped along England's single land frontier. Little as Englishmen liked being attached to either of the two great Powers, they could not very well avoid being bound to an extent to one or the other of them, since alone they would have succumbed to either; as they had discovered not long since that without Spain they could neither defend nor retake Calais. A visiting diplomat to the little island kingdom, summing up his impressions, compared it to " a bone thrown between two dogs."

The comparison was apt as far as it went, but it left two factors out of account. One was the bursting energy of the English people, who took by no means so gloomy a view of their future as the facts seemed to justify. The other was their new Queen, on whom they had increasingly fixed their faith as things went from bad to worse under her predecessor. So great had her popularity grown before the end that, not

not only had Mary not dared to prevent, but had been compelled against her will to consent to her accession, which her subjects welcomed with an enthusiasm that was almost hysterical. For one thing they liked the look of her: her tall, easy carriage, the shrewd look in her blue eyes and the humorous set of her small firm mouth, the vitality that radiated from her glistening red hair and pale olive skin. They delighted in her quick repartee, often exchanged in public with even the humblest of her subjects without in the least compromising her dignity, and smiled at the vanity which caused her to dress more gorgeously than any queen had ever dressed before, and to demand admiration from all beholders for her skill in dancing and the beauty of her long white hands. In many ways, far more than Edward or Mary had done, she reminded people of her father who, despite his many evil deeds, remained in memory as the masterful figure of what a king really ought to be.

But though like him in certain outward respects, in her gift of popularity and her unconcealed love of ruling, she soon showed herself quite unlike him in others no less important. Henry had been aggressive, extravagant, high-handed. From the very beginning Elizabeth preferred the methods of patience, compromise and thrift—perhaps because of the dangers which she had undergone in her youth, which Henry, as Prince of Wales admired by all the world, had been spared. Henry had overturned the ancient Church and substituted another with himself as Supreme Head; or, as others would maintain, declared its independence and reformed it. In either event he had carried the change through with brutal violence, killing many of his best subjects, dividing the rest and provoking further changes and reactions until it seemed that England would never again enjoy peace. Elizabeth, confronted with the latest change, the re-union with Rome under Mary, began by conforming to it despite the expectation of those who had most ardently desired her accession that she would immediately revoke it. Very carefully, with aid of statesmen and churchmen, she sought a compromise which would be acceptable to the largest possible number of people of different beliefs, and in the end arrived at a settlement sufficiently satisfactory to have lasted in nearly all its essentials to the present day.

The same prudence assisted her to achieve, if not altogether a satisfactory, at least a sensible ending to the war with France. To acknowledge that Calais had permanently passed to the French would have been a serious blow to Elizabeth's prestige in the eyes of her subjects, who remembered that not long since Henry had conquered and for a while held Boulogne as well. But to attempt to reconquer it without calling, and thereby admitting dependence, upon Spanish help was for the present impossible, and would at any time have required a large expenditure of lives and money and left France a permanent enemy. So a treaty of peace was agreed upon and Calais, without being formally declared French, allowed to remain in French hands on condition of a substantial sum being paid to England within a stated period. English pride was thus spared, at least in part, and France converted from an enemy to a potential and most useful friend in the years to come. Meanwhile, instead of squandering money she did not possess on a war she could not hope to win, Elizabeth continued with the aid of her very able agent in Antwerp, Sir Thomas Gresham, to borrow enough for her current needs and to be able, with the exercise of strict economy, to buy back the debased coinage and within a couple of years to put English currency on a sound footing again—in the end making an actual profit out of the operation for her Treasury as well.

In all this she was served by the very remarkable body of ministers who composed her Privy Council. At their head, where he was to remain for forty years, stood Sir William Cecil, her Principal Secretary, a man peculiarly qualified to represent her and the age which was for ever to be identified with her name. At thirty-eight he already had the

wide experience of public affairs which she necessarily
lacked and could only gain with time, having been
Secretary to Somerset and even after the Protector's
fall an important member of the highest political
circles; it was to him, as principal organiser of her
supporters behind the scenes, that she largely owed
her smooth accession to the throne. A Protestant,
though a moderate one, he belonged to the group
of Cambridge intellectuals which during the last
two-thirds of the sixteenth century increasingly
dominated not only English religion and government, but education, thought and letters as well.
Representative of the same trend of thought, and of
the new ruling class which embodied it, was his
brother-in-law, the Lord Keeper of the Seal, Sir
Nicholas Bacon, father of the great Sir Francis who
would one day take his place as the chief law officer
of the Crown.

But though they and others of similar convictions,
like the former treasurer of Elizabeth's household,
Sir Thomas Parry, wielded the principal influence
in the new Queen's government, they did not, like a
modern cabinet, completely control it. For they
were responsible not to a Parliamentary majority
but directly to her; and from the very beginning
she was resolved not to allow any particular group
of advisers to have absolute sway. Great changes
there had to be, since that was what her people, or

a large part of them, expected of her after the
disastrous results of Mary's acts and policies. But
many if not most were also frightened of great change,
as people generally are, even if in principle they feel
them to be necessary, and it was one of the marks
of Elizabeth's natural genius for ruling that from
the first she realised the importance of making great
changes look as little frightening as possible. Partly
she accomplished this by including in her Council
men of a more conservative sort than the Cecil
group, men who had served her father and her
sister, and would undoubtedly have included more
of their sort, both churchmen and laymen, had they
been willing to compromise. With them she included
still a third sort, men without any strong religious
convictions, administrators rather than politicians,
of whom the outstanding example was her Lord
Treasurer, the aged Marquess of Northampton, the
brother of Catherine Parr, whose long experience
extended back unbroken through the reigns of Mary,
Edward and Henry, and whose reform of the nation's
chaotic finances contributed greatly, along with
Elizabeth's own instinct for economy, to the astound-
ing results obtained by England with its comparatively small resources against rivals far richer.

Of these the most dangerous was still France; for
though peace had been restored on the Continent by
the Treaty signed in the spring of 1559, another

threat remained even nearer home. Two months
after the signature of the Treaty the French King
died as the result of an accident in a tourney and
was succeeded by his son the Dauphin as Francis II.
The wife of Francis, Mary Stuart, thereby became
Queen of France as well as of Scotland. By most
of Catholic Europe, which had never accepted
Elizabeth as legitimate, she was considered to be
also the rightful Queen of England. She so considered herself; and it was plainly but a matter of
time before she would put forward her claim with
French support. With her mother, a French
Princess, reigning for her in Edinburgh and a French
army stationed along the almost undefended Anglo-
Scottish frontier, it was easy to envisage an invasion
by land from the north accompanied by a French
landing by sea from the south.

Very much alive to this danger, Elizabeth's
ministers urged her to anticipate it by invading first,
with the object of expelling the French and setting
up a government in Scotland favourable to England,
which in the circumstances meant a government of
Protestants. She did not like taking the risks nor
spending the money a war would involve; nor did
she like inciting the subjects of a fellow-Queen to
rebellion, thus setting an example which might be
used against herself. But Mary positively challenged
her by incorporating the royal arms of England

with her own, to show that she regarded herself as their rightful possessor. A powerful group of Scots under her half-brother the Earl of Murray raised a Protestant rebellion and invited Elizabeth to take Scotland under her protection. It was an opportunity not to be missed, and presently an English army, after some hard fighting, reached Edinburgh, where Cecil in person concluded a Treaty obliging the French to withdraw their forces and the Queen of Scots to abandon the use of Elizabeth's arms.

Little more than two years had elapsed since the bitter mid-winter of England's defeat at Calais. Now, in the early summer of 1560, the same formidable enemy had been driven clean out of the British Isles. Scotland, the foe in countless murderous battles, had been won to friendship and the peril from that side could for the present be considered over. Meanwhile the measures taken to restore the country's unity and prosperity had already begun to lift it out of its previous gloom and give it an exhilarating feeling of strength and hope. For all this the people looked with admiration and gratitude to their young Queen, to whom they gave the largest share of the credit. Even her severest critic, the Spanish ambassador, who approved of almost nothing that she did, admitted that she was the real ruler and no mere tool in her ministers' hands:

" She seems to me," he wrote, " incomparably more feared than her sister, and gives her orders and has her way as absolutely as her father did." In fact the principal difference between her admirers and her critics was that the former put her success so far down to cleverness, the latter to luck.

But on one point all were agreed, that it could not go on: that a woman ruling alone was a freak of nature who must sooner or later come to grief. In most countries she would not have been allowed to rule at all, it being universally felt that only a man could have the strength of mind and will to defend the Crown successfully against enemies at home and abroad; and though the law of England was exceptional in permitting a woman ruler, Henry VIII had done everything in his power to avert the accession of one, and the English people felt reason to regret that in Mary's case he had failed. Moreover, even if Elizabeth turned out different from Mary, there remained the problem of the succession. An unmarried Queen could not have an heir, and without an heir the country would be doomed at Elizabeth's death to the agony of a Civil War until the strongest should seize the Crown; as her grandfather Henry VII had done at the end of the Wars of the Roses, which the very old still remembered with horror. " Everything," declared the Spanish ambassador, " depends on the husband this woman chooses," and in that he expressed the opinion of all—ministers, Parliament and people—to whom the future of England mattered.

To this opinion there appeared to be only one dissenting voice—Elizabeth's own. At her coronation she had declared that she never intended to marry, that only England should be her husband. It was prettily said, but no one really believed it; for even if she thought herself capable of ruling without a man's help and guidance, she could hardly show herself indifferent to the country's need of a prince of her blood to succeed her when she died. Amongst those who refused to believe it were a dozen or so gentlemen who almost immediately proposed to her. Some of them were her subjects, like the Earl of Arundel, a great nobleman, and Sir William Pickering, a great ladies' man; the others represented practically all the ruling Houses of Europe from Sweden to Spain. As time went on and her fame, as well as the power and importance of England in world affairs, increased, the number of her suitors also increased, until the list included, simultaneously or in turn, her brother-in-law Philip II of Spain, his two Austrian Hapsburgh cousins, the sons of the Holy Roman Emperor, a King of France, Charles IX, and his two brothers, a King of Sweden, a Prince of Denmark, a mixed array of Dukes, and— a little doubtfully—a Russian Czar.

Most of these, it will be noticed, were Catholics, but her loyal, and vociferously Protestant, Lords and Commons, were so anxious for her to marry somebody, anybody, that they were willing for her, they often desperately urged her, to marry even a papist so long as he was satisfied to practise his religion in private. To all of her suitors, whether they proposed by ambassador or came in person, Elizabeth gave a warm welcome, listened to what they had to say, and herself never said either yes or no. Her people wondered. Sometimes they grew angry with her, and she with them; once she had a quarrel with her House of Commons, when they urged her to get on with it, so serious that she nearly sent one especially outspoken member to prison, but wisely thought better of it. Though few if any took seriously her assertion that she really preferred to remain single, some suspected that she might have a deep, unnatural aversion to married life which she would not disclose to any one. There were, however, perfectly rational reasons for her hesitation: if she married a Spaniard or an Austrian she would, like her sister before her, have made an enemy of France, if a Frenchman an enemy of the Austro-Spanish group; if she married a Protestant she might align both the great Catholic Powers against her; while if she tried to play safe from foreign entanglements by marrying an Englishman, she might easily make

enemies of other subjects who would object to her
husband being raised above them. But many felt
then, and have felt since, that the real, or at least
a most important reason, why she would not marry,
though every consideration for her country demanded
that she should, was that she was already in love
with a man whom it was impossible for her to marry.

The name of the man was Lord Robert Dudley,
and he was the son of the Duke of Northumberland
who had tried to keep Mary from her throne. Had
Robert not already been married when he was
eighteen to a girl named Amy Robsart, his father
might well have married him instead of his younger
brother to Lady Jane Grey, in which case he would
long since have been dead. As it was he was actually
sentenced to death for his part in his father's plot,
but was let off by Mary after a year in the Tower,
where Elizabeth was a prisoner at the same time
and was said by some to have met and fallen in
love with him. Later he went abroad to fight in
France, and on his return joined the party which
was trying to make sure of Elizabeth's accession on
Mary's death and sold lands to help her with money
in case of need. When she became Queen she made
him her Master of the Horse, a picturesque and
profitable office which kept him constantly near her.
Very soon the gossip about the two began. He was
about Elizabeth's age, a man of exceedingly hand-

some presence, tall and dark, with the fine figure of a born athlete and the smooth, ready tongue of the born courtier. Some men, and many women, admired him, but the people in general hated him, partly because of his family's reputation as crooked and greedy upstarts, partly because of his haughty pride and his influence over the Queen, which some attributed to an unholy spell he had cast over her. Though Elizabeth always stoutly denied that she treated him better than his merits deserved, her unconcealed delight in his company and the offices and gifts she lavished on him naturally caused resentment and wonder that a man whose qualities few respected should by her favour alone have become one of the richest and most powerful in the land. It was not as if she could marry him: this in itself made his intimacy with Elizabeth scandalous enough, a cause of shame to her adoring people. But even worse was feared, namely that in order to satisfy his supreme ambition to share her crown he would not hesitate to get rid of his wife somehow or other; and many a patriotic Englishman said outright that it would be an excellent thing if he were to disappear from the world before that happened.

This was the situation when Cecil returned from Edinburgh in the summer of 1560 after concluding the victorious treaty with the French. Instead of finding the universal rejoicing he expected at England's triumph, he found the Court and the country seething with rumours of impending disaster, and the Queen haggard and fretful. Shortly afterwards, on the eve of her twenty-seventh birthday, September 7th, which that year fell on a Saturday, the Spanish Ambassador came to Windsor Castle, where the Court was in residence, to clear up certain points regarding Elizabeth's marriage with the Austrian Archduke, which was then under discussion. In the course of a private conference with Cecil the latter suddenly burst out that the Queen was so far gone in love with Robert that she was neglecting her business and in a fair way to ruining the country; that Robert and his friends were spreading reports to the effect that his wife, then living at Cumnor, near Oxford, was fatally ill of cancer, but that this was not true, and that he, Cecil, knew she was taking good care not to be poisoned; and finally repeated with bitter emphasis twice over that it would be better if Lord Robert were removed to another world. Fascinated by this outburst from the Queen's chief minister, ordinarily the most self-controlled as well as the best-informed of men, the Ambassador hastened to report it to his direct superior, Philip II's sister Margaret, whom he had left as Regent of the Netherlands on his departure for Spain the previous year. The letter had not yet been finished and sent off before a messenger arrived from Cumnor with the news, which the Ambassador heard from Elizabeth's own lips next day, that at noon of Sunday the 8th Robert's wife had been found with her neck broken at the bottom of a flight of stairs.

Precisely what happened no one will ever know. Robert immediately sent a confidential servant to Cumnor with orders for the most thorough investigation and the punishment of the guilty, if any were found, whoever they might be. On the servant's arrival he found the coroner's jury, sober and substantial men of the neighbourhood, already assembled and a few days later they brought in a verdict of death by misadventure—presumably a stumble on the stairs ending on the stone flags below. The servant seems to have thought differently; at least the evidence he gathered for Robert pointed in quite another direction. His late mistress, according to the testimony of her maid, who loved her dearly, had for some time been in great distress and had often been seen on her knees praying to God to save her from desperation. On the fatal morning she had, according to several witnesses, ordered every one in the house to go to the fair being held in the nearby town of Abingdon and quarrelled with a lady companion who refused to leave her. A distraught woman, anxious to be left alone in a large house, strongly suggested an intention of suicide, and quite likely poor Amy Dudley, living an aimless existence apart from her husband, conscious of standing in the way of his advancement, perhaps really suffering from cancer as rumoured—quite likely she decided to take this way out.

But very few believed it, any more than they believed the coroner's jury. Even Robert himself seems not to have believed it, for he continued to search for a murderer; and Sir Walter Scott was apparently of Robert's way of thinking, because in his novel *Kenilworth* he attributes Amy's death to a couple of Robert's retainers acting in their master's supposed interests unbeknown to him. But the important thing from Robert and Elizabeth's point of view was that her people, hating him and seeing how strong a motive he had for wishing his wife dead, assumed without further argument that he was in fact responsible for her being dead. Could they have had their way they would have killed him or driven him from the kingdom; not only because they hated him but because they loved Elizabeth, and were terrified lest she now marry him and in so doing proclaim to all the world that she had all along, as her enemies were not slow to proclaim, been associated in his crime. From all sides, from preachers in their pulpits, from her diplomats abroad, came desperate pleas not to marry Robert but to get rid of him altogether lest he disgrace and ruin her. Get rid of him she would not, because she loved him and firmly believed in his innocence. But she also realised, with the cool good sense which was so fundamental a part of her, that she could not marry him. Her people's love would be turned to hate, their faith in her innocence into conviction of her guilt. So she kept him by her, went on favouring him and in time made good use of him.

And so she saved herself from the tragic fate of the next important character in her story, her young Scottish cousin Mary Stuart, who for love's sake was presently to commit the blunder Elizabeth had avoided and in so doing involve Elizabeth in the most painful problem of her life.

History
102

# * 3 *

## The Scottish Cousin

---

NINE YEARS younger than Elizabeth, Mary Stuart had been Queen of Scotland almost from the day she was born, her father, King James V, having not long survived his last battle with the English at Solway Moss. Through her grandmother Margaret, elder sister of Henry VIII and wife of King James IV, she was also born with a claim on the throne of England next after Henry VIII's own children's: in fact, better than that of her two girl cousins, Mary and Elizabeth, whom the law as it then stood debarred from the succession. This law, however, Henry later caused to be amended so as not only to restore his daughters to their rightful place but to set aside the descendants of his elder sister in favour of the younger, another Mary, Duchess of Suffolk, on the ground that the former, being Scots, were foreigners. So unusual a departure from what was customary struck most people, however, as illegal and improper, and when the granddaughter of the

Duchess of Suffolk, Lady Jane Grey, became involved in Northumberland's plot, public opinion generally granted that should Elizabeth die childless, historic custom would be honoured and Mary Stuart succeed her. Henry himself had hoped to avoid all these complications by arranging a marriage between the Scottish Queen and his heir, Edward VI, so as to unite the two realms under one crown, and had tried to bully the Scots into consenting by the threat of invasion. He had failed, and the Protector Somerset, who later had the same idea, failed also, for as his army advanced over the Border the infant Queen was hastily carried off to France.

There she was brought up at the French Court as a French child and when she was fifteen married to the young Dauphin, who the next year succeeded his father as Francis II. So Mary Stuart was Queen of France as well, while her mother, a French Princess of the great House of Guise, reigned for her as Regent in Edinburgh. How as a result French troops garrisoned Scotland and Elizabeth drove them out has already been told.

Only a few months after this, in December, 1560, Francis II died and was succeeded by his nine-year-old brother Charles IX. Mary, just arrived at her eighteenth birthday, had to decide what to do with her future. In France, which she loved, she could no longer expect happiness because the young King's mother, Catherine de Medici, who now became the real ruler, disliked and distrusted her. Scotland, on the other hand, Mary had not known since she was a small child, and should she return to it would find herself a complete stranger there, with the government in the hands of men hostile to herself and to all that she had been brought up to believe: a Catholic and a Frenchwoman confronted with Protestants set in power by English arms. Finally she decided that she preferred being Queen in her native country to being a nobody in her adopted one, and asked Elizabeth for permission to pass through England on her way to Scotland. Elizabeth refused; Mary had never abandoned the use of the English arms, as provided in the Treaty of Edinburgh: many in England, especially in certain Catholic circles, believed she had a better right to them than Elizabeth and might feel dangerously moved by her youth and beauty, which her sorrowful widow's dress much enhanced, if they actually saw her. So Mary had to take ship and run the risks of the North Sea fogs and the prowling seamen who infested it before she safely reached Edinburgh in August, 1561.

Despite Elizabeth's resentment at Mary's use of her arms, and Mary's at Elizabeth's refusal to allow her a safe-conduct through England, the two cousins tried for a while to be friends. It is unlikely that they could ever have succeeded; Mary was too jealous of Elizabeth as the greater Queen, Elizabeth of Mary as the younger and more attractive woman about whose charms so many men, some of them poets, were always bursting into rapture; Elizabeth represented a constant obstacle to Mary's ambitions, Mary to Elizabeth's security. Nevertheless for a while they really tried to come to an understanding. Affectionate letters and costly presents passed between them, and for many months they planned a meeting at which they would chat, sew and play music together in order to get thoroughly to know each other. But the meeting had to be put off because Elizabeth got involved in a civil war in France, where she took the side of the Protestant Huguenots against the Catholics and suffered a defeat, in part because of a plague that ravaged her troops; and though Mary acted well, refraining from taking advantage of the Queen of England's difficulties, even though Elizabeth was fighting against her Guise relatives, when the war was over other complications prevented the plans for the meeting from being discussed again. For by that time Mary was making other plans and the struggle was beginning which would not end until one of the cousins was dead.

If Elizabeth was the best match in Europe, Mary was the next best; and the ruling Houses that had so far had poor success with England were not long in directing their attention to Scotland. Philip II offered his son and heir, Don Carlos, the Holy Roman Emperor the Archduke Charles, whom he had already offered to Elizabeth, even Catherine de Medici was willing to have Mary once more as a daughter-in-law, as wife to Charles IX, rather than have her marry a Spaniard or an Austrian. Any of these marriages would have been welcome to Mary insofar as it would have increased her prestige and importance. But for the same reason they were all intolerable to Elizabeth, since they would have given one of the great continental Powers a foothold in Scotland and an interest in pressing Mary's claim to the English throne. It was the very situation she had fought a war at the beginning of her reign to put an end to, and would if necessary, as she warned Mary, fight another. Mary could not but heed the warning, since Elizabeth was the stronger, and the Scots were in any event not likely to fight in order to enable her to marry a Catholic prince.

Furious with Elizabeth, she became even more furious at another and very different kind of marriage which Elizabeth proposed instead. From Elizabeth's point of view the most suitable husband for Mary was one on whose loyalty she could count to keep Scotland from doing anything hurtful to England, and with that in mind she offered Mary the most

intimate of her friends and counsellors, Robert
Dudley, whom she had just made Earl of Leicester.
Mary's feelings may be imagined: after being
warned that she might not marry any Prince whom
she considered worthy of her, now to be told that
she might have a man whose father and grandfather
had been condemned traitors, one whom Elizabeth
herself had been compelled to refuse (as was generally
believed) because of the suspicion that he was a
murderer. But after one outburst Mary kept her
temper, as befitted a Queen, and asked Elizabeth
whether, if she married Leicester, she would be
solemnly assured by law of the succession to the
English throne—the supreme desire of her life to
which all else was secondary. Quite possibly
Elizabeth would have liked to say yes, but she did
not dare to. It was far from certain that Parliament,
however much it might urge her to name a successor,
would accept a Catholic. It was more than certain
that if one were named a great party would form
round him or her, dividing the nation, opposing and
enfeebling the policies of the Crown and for ever
thinking how much better it would be if the present
wearer were to be replaced by her successor. The
situation too vividly recalled to Elizabeth the danger
she herself had created for her sister; in her own
striking phrase to Parliament, to name an heir
would be like wearing her own shroud before she

was dead. So she promised Mary to do her best for her if she married Leicester but would give no legal guarantee. This was not enough for Mary, who in any case did not want Leicester and had already thought out another way of getting what she did want.

We have already seen that Henry VIII tried to bar the Scottish Stuarts from the throne because they were foreigners. This, and their religion, made them unacceptable to a large part of the English people. But there were also English Stuarts, a junior branch of the same family, of whom the chief was Mary's slightly younger cousin Lord Darnley. If she were to marry him, it occurred to her, they would as a wedded pair retain the advantage of being next-of-kin while overcoming the disadvantage of being foreigners. Mary caused Darnley to apply for permission to come to Scotland in order to look after some property he had there. Elizabeth, with the hearty approval of her ministers, refused: Mary's intention was too transparent. But when Darnley renewed his application, Elizabeth, this time to the horror of her ministers, granted it. It almost looked as if she wanted Mary to marry Darnley, foreseeing what would come of it. This in fact was what the envoy whom she presently sent to Scotland to forbid the marriage thought when he discovered that he had been sent too late. For by then Darnley had arrived, had been found by Mary to be a good-looking, graceful young man, and had aroused her sympathy by falling gravely ill. By the time Elizabeth's order forbidding the marriage arrived it had already taken place. To the world it looked as if she had been out-manœuvred and out-witted.

But what came of it was very different from what Mary had supposed; perhaps, after all, Elizabeth had judged the bridegroom better. He turned out to be greedy, vicious and untrustworthy, thinking little of Mary and everything of himself. Her early affection was soon displaced by dislike and contempt, and having nowhere else to look for comfort and help, since the government in Edinburgh was dominated by men opposed to her in politics and religion, she took for her chief friend and adviser an Italian musician named David Rizzio. Darnley of course immediately hated and was jealous of him. With some accomplices, including several of Mary's ministers, who also hated Rizzio, he organised a plot which resulted in Rizzio's being stabbed to death at Holyrood Palace in Mary's very presence. The further purpose of the plot was to put Mary under constraint and make Darnley to all intents King. But Mary, by remarkable resourcefulness and courage, managed to estrange him from his confederates and completely turn the tables on him. Soon she regained control of her capital, from which she had for a time prudently slipped away. The following June, 1566, she achieved her moment of greatest triumph when she gave birth to a future King not only of Scotland but, as many at once recognised, in all probability of England as well. To that extent she had calculated the results of her marriage soundly, if not for herself then at least for the baby James her son.

But the moment of triumph was short. She felt herself terribly alone, surrounded on all sides by enemies to her ambitions and her faith. The temptation came to her to ally her fortunes with those of a reckless adventurer, James Hepburn, Earl of Bothwell, a man of no party and no certain religion. Some say, on the strength of a collection of verses and letters purporting to have been written by her to him, that she fell desperately in love with him; others hold that the letters and verses are in whole or part forgeries; but it is hard to deny that her actions resembled those of a woman prepared to go almost any lengths for a man's sake. Bothwell, though already married, could, and did, divorce his wife. Darnley was a more difficult problem, among other reasons because to Mary as a Catholic divorce was forbidden. Fearing for his life Darnley had left the capital for Glasgow, then still a country village, where he fell ill of smallpox. Mary went to him, offered to be reconciled, nursed him until he was better and brought him back to Edinburgh. There, on the night of February 9th, 1567, after he had gone to bed and she out to a party, a terrific explosion wrecked the building in which he was staying, and he and his page were found dead in the garden outside—killed, according to some reports, not by the explosion but by strangling before it occurred.

Little as Darnley was liked, the crime so shocked and horrified the Scottish people that they set up an instant cry for inquiry and punishment. Mary's situation was in some respects like Elizabeth's after the death of Amy Dudley, in others far worse. No one ever doubted, then or since, that her lover had caused the murder of her husband to clear the way for their marriage. In similar circumstances Elizabeth had sent Dudley from Court into private arrest until the coroner's jury had completed its investigation, after which she was able to quote its verdict in Dudley's defence. This Mary could not have done, even if she had wanted to. For one thing, too many of the principal men in her kingdom, some of them driven into exile as the result of Darnley's deserting and betraying them after Rizzio's death, had at the very least approved, and perhaps abetted Bothwell's plot to kill him. For another, Mary could not control Bothwell as Elizabeth had been able to control Dudley. When Darnley's father, from England, accused him of the murder and demanded

a trial, Bothwell was able to frighten the old man
into staying away from Scotland and then to terrify
the judges charged with hearing the evidence into
acquitting him. Worse was soon to follow. With a
party of horsemen he waylaid Mary on a highroad,
carried her off and married her before a Protestant
minister. Not many believed that he had done it
against her will, or believed henceforth that she had
not known in advance of his intention to murder
Darnley.

Her married life was short and wretchedly un-
happy. Bothwell bullied and tormented her so that
only two days after the wedding she was heard to
wish that she were dead; yet she continued to adore
him. When the people of Edinburgh shouted to her
face that she was an adulteress and murderess, she
answered them back with spirit. But her enemies
and Bothwell's, taking advantage of the popular
feeling, rose against them, drove him into hiding
and imprisoned her in an island fortress. There she
remained for nearly a year while her captors argued
about the conditions of her release. They had the
physical advantage of power, but she still had the
advantage of being their lawful Queen; however
dreadful the crimes of which she was suspected, it
was considered no less dreadful of them to have
rebelled against the Lord's anointed to whom their
sworn loyalty belonged.

It was this last point that most forcibly shook Elizabeth, who naturally took the view that it was wrong in any circumstances for subjects to turn against their sovereign. From the first she believed, or acted as if she did, that Mary was innocent of Darnley's murder, but that she should have it thoroughly looked into and have whoever was guilty punished, even if it proved to be Bothwell. But to this Mary would not agree, for the reasons given above. At the same time Elizabeth severely reprimanded the Scots lords, even though most of them were pro-English, for their acts of violence against their Queen. But the lords dared not heed her; if they now let Mary go free, under whatever conditions, they felt sure she would seek help both at home and abroad, which she might well succeed in obtaining, in order to regain her power and revenge herself upon them for what they had done to her. They had the bear by the tale—or, as it was put in those days, the wolf by the ears—and dared not let go for fear lest she turn and destroy them. And even while those discussions were going on, Mary cut them short with her usual vigour and daring by escaping from her prison, joining Bothwell and raising an army to lead to battle against her enemies. But once more she was defeated: Bothwell fled to Denmark, whence he never returned, and Mary, with no alternative but recapture and probable death, fled across the border into England.

It was the last thing Elizabeth wanted. For whatever she now did was certain to be dangerous and to put her in the wrong. Mary at once wrote asking for her hospitality; she could not very well refuse it to a fellow human being, let alone a fellow Queen, in mortal peril. But to let her roam free meant that those of Elizabeth's subjects who longed to see her succeed—some of them even to replace—Elizabeth would gather round her, as in fact they immediately began to do, be charmed by her, pity her, desire to help her. If Mary did not persuade them to help her turn Elizabeth out—always a possibility—she might well persuade them to help her recover Scotland, thus involving Elizabeth either in a war with the Scots or with those of her own people who followed Mary. To send her back to Scotland amounted, as things were, to sending her to certain death; to force the Scots to take her back could only be done by force, which would be no better if undertaken by the English Crown than by Mary's English admirers.

In order to give herself time to think, Elizabeth had Mary kept under restraint in a castle in the North. But this was doing the very thing she had scolded the Scots lords for doing, namely imprisoning an anointed Queen; and Mary, quick to perceive

Elizabeth's difficulty, haughtily demanded to be set free to go to France and seek more trustworthy friends there. But this Elizabeth could not allow either, for if Mary brought back a French or any other continental army to restore her to her throne, Elizabeth would for her own safety have to expel it by force as she had done before. The only solution that occurred to her was much the same as the one she had attempted when Mary was a prisoner in Scotland the year before, namely to reach a compromise with the Scottish lords whereby Mary would be restored to her throne under sufficient guarantees both for their and England's safety.

So the Lords were summoned to York, in appearance as rebels to answer before a group of Elizabeth's ministers their Queen's complaints against them. But instead of confining themselves to this role, they insisted on the Englishmen hearing their complaints against her: for Bothwell had left behind him in his flight a silver casket containing the poems and letters, previously referred to, which Mary had written him and which appeared to prove, not only that she had been in love with Bothwell while married to Darnley, but had known in advance of Bothwell's intention to murder him. Mary and her defenders denounced the contents of the casket as forgeries, and a complicated dispute arose which caused the proceedings to be transferred to Westminster. There Mary, through her representatives, refused to answer the accusations against her at all, proudly asserting that a Queen could not be put on trial whatever she might have done. To this Elizabeth could not but in principle agree. But in practice she could hardly require the Scots to take back a Queen whom they claimed on the evidence of her own writings to have proved guilty of a murder. And so things remained as they were, and Mary stayed on in England a prisoner, hoping and planning until, many years later, the final terrible solution of her problem was found.

Meanwhile her presence in England marked the end of Elizabeth's first ten years of comparative peace and the beginning of the troubles which brought on the first great crisis of her reign, the greatest until the Spanish Armada twenty years later threatened England's shores and her very existence as a nation.

# * 4 *
## Rebellion

To FIND the underlying cause of the troubles which henceforth beset Elizabeth one must look back to the fifteen years or so before she was born. Before that time, for a thousand years and more, the peoples of Europe had fought about many things, but they had been united in believing one thing: that there existed a single " Holy, Catholic and Apostolic Church " of which the Bishop of Rome, under the title of the Pope, was the visible and recognisable head in succession to St. Peter. But in 1517 a German monk, Martin Luther, had challenged certain Catholic teachings and renounced his obedience to the papacy. Others had followed him, including Henry VIII and a French lawyer named John Calvin, who had gone even further in his repudiation of Catholic belief and gained many disciples in many lands. In some of them, like England, Scotland and various of the little Germanic states, whole kingdoms had broken away under the leadership of their secular rulers; in others which had remained predominantly Catholic, like France, the Low Countries and Poland, part of the population had joined one or another of the dissenting churches and were prepared to fight rather than return to their former allegiance to Rome.

Thus Europe was divided in every which way, the southern and eastern two-thirds still Catholic, the northern and western one-third what was coming to be called Protestant, though English-ruled Ireland remained solidly Catholic and the Spanish-ruled Netherlands, particularly the northern part approximating to modern Holland, grew increasingly Protestant; while in virtually every country, whether officially Catholic or Protestant, those of the contrary faith fiercely attempted to convert their neighbours and equally fiercely resisted their neighbours' attempts to convert them. For this there was no simple, friendly solution to be reached on the principle of live-and-let-live. Each party believed that it had hold of the truth, the only truth that mattered, the one that led to eternal salvation, and that its adversaries clung to falsehood which must necessarily lead to eternal damnation: not only for themselves but for all who should permit them to survive and infect others with their errors. Toleration, even reasonable discussion, was impossible. God and the devil could not mix. Just as Elizabeth

Q.E. F

was to ardent Catholics " that Jezebel," so to earnest Protestants the Pope was " that wolfish bloodsucker," and their Catholic fellow-creatures mad dogs, toads and other such vermin to be cleansed off the face of the earth.

These feelings, dangerous enough in themselves, were made more so by questions of geography and money. The Catholic countries bordering on the Mediterranean were by far the richest. From the beginning of the Middle Ages the Republic of Venice had controlled the trade routes to the East, bringing the wares carried out of Persia, China and the Indies by camel to her depots in Syria and reloading them in her high, gorgeously painted vessels for transhipment to Italy and beyond. Since the end of the fifteenth century, first Portugal by sailing round Africa to India, then Spain by the discovery of America, had likewise been in a position to bring for sale to Europe all the rare and wonderful things for which Europe longed—silks and precious woods, sugar and spices, gold and silver, works of exquisite art and strange animals from peacocks to tigers. In 1494, two years after Columbus's first voyage to America, Pope Alexander VI had divided the unexplored world beyond the seas between Spain and Portugal as a reward for their enterprise and to keep them from fighting. The other countries had respected this division so long as they remained

Catholic; but presently it occurred to the English that since they no longer obeyed the Pope's orders in spiritual matters, there was no reason any longer to do so in others. So in the early years of Elizabeth's reign some of her seamen, notably Sir John Hawkins and his young cousin Francis Drake, carried negro slaves from West Africa to the Spanish territories in Central America and the West Indies, where the local planters were glad to buy them; and sometimes, when the local Spanish governors protested, even landed them at the cannon's mouth. The Spaniards retaliated, in one instance with deadly effect, on Hawkins's ships and men off the coast of Mexico. In return the English got their own, and more than their own, back by raiding Spanish ships on their way home with the treasure of Mexico and Peru, on the ground that the Spaniards had no exclusive claim to the treasure, and that anyhow it was a virtue to spoil the idolaters, as the Chosen People in the Bible had despoiled the Egyptians. This feeling grew even stronger when, towards the middle of Elizabeth's reign, Spain annexed Portugal and thus laid claim to a world-wide monopoly which would have prevented any one else from lawfully carrying on trade across the oceans anywhere at all.

Meanwhile the relations of religious and trading interests had started trouble nearer home. For a long time England had been the friend of Spain and the enemy of France for two important reasons. One was that France, being nearer and militarily stronger, was the more dangerous; the other was that England's chief business was carried on with the Low Countries, a Spanish dominion, which took the bulk of England's main export, wool, and repaid in things that England wanted, such as linens, cloths of silver and gold, dye-stuffs, salt and many other articles. These were brought down the Rhine by barge from the interior of the Continent. Moreover, in Antwerp, the largest banking centre of northern Europe, the English Government and merchants were in the habit of raising loans.

But in the Netherlands there had arisen, as already stated, a stong Protestant movement. The Spanish Government began, a few years after Elizabeth's accession, to try to stamp it out. The Netherlanders, especially the Dutch of the northern Provinces, turned rebellious; many fled for safety from persecution to England, where their sufferings provoked strong sympathy amongst their co-religionists, and a corresponding anger against Spain. This feeling increased when Hawkins returned to report the attack—by treachery, as he alleged—against him in Mexico. At this moment some Genoese ships carrying gold which Philip II had borrowed in Italy to pay his troops in the Low Countries put in to a Channel port to evade some pirates lying in wait for them outside. The English authorities seized the gold and brought it to London; when Spain asked for it back, Elizabeth answered that since it was only a loan, she herself would assume responsibility for it to the lenders. Naturally the Spaniards were furious at what they called barefaced robbery, and all the more furious because they feared that if the troops engaged in suppressing the Dutch rebellion were not paid they would mutiny. Which is what presently happened and perhaps what Elizabeth and her advisers hoped would happen. When the Spaniards, to punish her, seized the goods of English merchants in the Netherlands, she retorted by seizing the property of the Netherlands merchants in England; and since this happened to be the greater, the Spaniards were forced to heed the outcry of their angry subjects and try for a peaceable settlement of the matter.

We have heard a great deal in our day of " cold war," war in which the antagonists injure one another in every way possible without openly fighting. This sort of war England and Spain now conducted off and on for twenty years. Neither Elizabeth nor Philip II wanted to go any further. He had enough on his hands already, what with the rebellion of his Dutch provinces and the constant threat of the Turks and the Moors to his commerce in the Medi-

terranean; despite his great wealth he was always
desperately short of ready money for his immediate
needs. Elizabeth on her side hated war with all her
might, deeming it wasteful, risky and pointless. This
feeling of hers can hardly be exaggerated; it is the
principal key to her character and conduct as a
statesman. Unlike her father, and most kings of his
time, she had no desire for military glory; what she
desired was that her country should be safe, peaceful
and prosperous. She had solemnly declared at the
time of her coronation that England was her husband,
and her attitude was very much that of wife and
mother to a large and active family. Like a good
housekeeper she tried to keep expenses down and
live within her means, which were very small compared with those of the French or Spanish king—
normally only about £200,000 a year from lands, the
customs, etc., to cover all expenses of the Court and
the Government. Anything beyond this—armies,
navies, fortresses—required special taxes, which she
hated imposing almost as much as her people hated
paying them, and which she could ask for only at
the risk of diminishing her popularity and power.
If the men of the family—the Drakes, Hawkinses,
Humphrey Gilberts—wanted fighting and adventure,
she was quite ready to let them go off and look for
it, provided they did so at their own expense and
without involving the rest of the family. She

admired, often encouraged and secretly helped them, and when possible without danger to the nation sought to protect them from their enemies; but if they got hurt, they understood that they were not to run to her for comfort, still less expect her to gamble with her people's fortunes in order to retrieve theirs. During the twenty years of un-declared conflict with Spain it was men like those just mentioned who held England's end up, bringing in much wealth, sometimes suffering serious loss themselves, while their brethren at home farmed, manufactured, traded or cultivated their minds and Elizabeth concentrated upon keeping them united amongst themselves and safe from foreign embroilments.

By no means all her subjects agreed with her. Some thought her niggardly, even cowardly, for not going further, some considered her reckless and dishonest for going as far as she did. The former, the out-and-out Protestants, urged that England should organise and lead a crusade to put down Spain everywhere—in the Netherlands, beyond the seas, in France by joining her enemies to attack her friends there—until Protestantism dominated Europe and Spain's wealth and possessions had been stripped from her. Amongst Elizabeth's ministers this view was represented at first mainly by Cecil, later even more strongly by Leicester while Cecil more often took the Queen's side. Their opponents, Catholic by belief and sympathy, took the extreme opposite view. In their eyes Spain was the upholder of the one true faith which they hoped England would yet return to, and regarded any injury to her as unjust and criminal. They hated Elizabeth's principal ministers, not only for urging a wrong policy upon her, but as upstarts, greedy and corrupt men who had newly forced and tricked their way to wealth and power and hoped to gain more of both by the aggression they now advocated.

These feelings were particularly strong in the North, a part of the country less populated, less developed and less rich than the South. There the people had never taken to the new religion, nor to the Tudor monarchy, which to them represented something distant and oppressive; their first loyalty was still given, as in feudal times, to the great local families like the Percies and the Nevilles, of whom the Earls of Northumberland and Westmorland were respectively the heads. Once already, in Henry VIII's time, they had risen in a rebellion known as the Pilgrimage of Grace because of the government's suppression of the monasteries. Now the same temper began to work in them as tales spread from castle to castle and farmhouse to farmhouse of the events which appeared to be leading to war with Spain—the attacks on Spanish ships, the interception of the gold, the seizure of the merchants' goods. . . . A new Spanish Ambassador had recently arrived, Don Guerau de Spes, a born plotter who disliked Elizabeth and increased the people's fears by rumours that she had given in completely to Cecil and his clique, that she intended to launch a violent attack on Catholics everywhere, at home as well as abroad, fasten the succession on some obscure and unwanted Protestant, and so forth. The coming of Mary Stuart raised the tension still higher. For she was the symbol of all their hopes for the future, the rightful heir who would on Elizabeth's death restore the old faith. Those who saw her—and all who could flocked to do so—were delighted with her charm and friendliness, and passed on their impressions to their neighbours. None would believe ill of her; the stories spread about her misdeeds in Scotland were scoffed at as the propaganda of her enemies, designed to deprive her of her rights to the throne. And when Elizabeth, instead of receiving her as her injured cousin and heir, continued to keep her in captivity, it was taken as another and convincing proof of the government's evil intent towards the old religion and those who cherished it.

Yet, with all their grievances, so horrifying was the idea of rebellion and so sacred the person of Majesty that these northern folk never really meditated taking up arms against their Queen. Like many other catastrophes in history, the one now about to occur arose largely out of accident and misunderstanding. During the conference at York, in October, 1568, when the Casket Letters were first produced, various people thought that a good solution for the whole problem of Mary Stuart would be to marry her to some Englishman loyal and strong enough to stand responsible for her good conduct if she were set free. The only name seriously put forward in this connection was that of the Duke of Norfolk, who was present as one of the English commissioners. As the premier peer of the realm, and the richest, he had great influence in the country, and was generally regarded as the leader of the conservative faction in the government opposed to Cecil.

Norfolk was both attracted and repelled by the suggestion. Mary's record, as he said, frightened him; on the other hand, to be the husband of the Queen of Scots, with the strong possibility of becoming one day King Consort of England, was a prospect certainly tempting to an ambitious and conceited man. On the whole he was more attracted than repelled, but he was afraid to say so to Elizabeth lest she should suspect him of scheming against her. His friends urged him to tell her quite frankly what was in his mind, assuring him that he would not find her as set against it as he supposed. Elizabeth herself, who usually knew far more about what was going on than anybody realised, twice gave him a strong hint, once accompanied by a friendly pinch on the ear, that she was quite prepared to listen to his confession; but he, instead of taking the hint, hastily insisted that he had nothing to confess so far as Mary was concerned, and thus made it inevitable that Elizabeth, who knew better, should henceforth distrust his word.

But by then he dared admit his thoughts about Mary less than ever, since his conscience in other respects was no longer clear. For he had become involved with the Spanish Ambassador and the northern earls, no particular friends of his, in a plot, a whole series of plots . . . to seize Cecil and have him beheaded, to cause Elizabeth to make good past injuries to Spain and reverse her whole policy toward that country, all leading up to her approving Norfolk's marriage with Mary and recognising Mary as her heir. These plots were not very well co-ordinated and defined. They depended largely for their success on help from Spain, not only in money but, should the occasion for the use of force arise, in men to be sent from the Netherlands. The Spanish Ambassador had promised such help, but the Spanish Governor in the Netherlands, who alone could give it, declined to do so until the plotters had by their own efforts established control over a large part of England so that his troops could land with safety. On the moral side, too, there was a vital need still remaining, a decree from the Pope releasing Elizabeth's subjects from their allegiance to her, since without it thousands who otherwise approved of Norfolk's design would hesitate to assist him against their lawful sovereign; and the Pope, though appealed to, had not yet spoken.

For these and similar reasons Norfolk hesitated, and sometimes wished himself well out of the whole thing. But he was in too far and too many people in with him. Frightened, anxious to find out how much Elizabeth knew, and still more what she would do about it, he slipped away from Court without permission. Elizabeth promptly ordered him to return; though she did not know all that he had been up to, she knew enough to want him safely under her eye. In a panic he fled still farther, to his estates in the county whose name he bore, where he would be surrounded by his partisans, and from there sent frantic messages to the northern earls to stop what they were doing, whatever it was. But Elizabeth's orders followed him to Norfolk, and when he pleaded illness she ordered him to come if he had to be carried; perhaps she remembered a time when her sister had ordered *her* to Court, and she had likewise pleaded illness.

Norfolk came and was transported by river to the Tower, amidst thousands of spectators standing on the banks in wonder and pity, unable to imagine what England's only Duke could have done to merit such treatment. Indeed, various of Elizabeth's ministers, including even Cecil, rather agreed with them, unable to believe their aristocratic colleague really guilty of high treason. But Elizabeth had a powerful feminine intuition, and a great deal of experience where treason was concerned, which served her better than proof; and when it raised its head to threaten the peace of her realm and the security of her throne, she could be as swift to act as she was slow in undertaking wars. Some proof against Norfolk came when his confederates on the outside tried to pass messages to him in prison. His warnings to the northern earls had meanwhile caused them to pause in their preparations but had not done anything to quiet the impatience of their followers. Elizabeth summoned the earls to Court to explain themselves. They were inclined to obey, but their wives and retainers restrained them, urging them to put all to the hazard now that Elizabeth was suspicious of them anyway. While they hesitated, the decision was taken out of their hands. Not the leaders—neither the earls nor Norfolk, nor Mary, nor the Spanish Ambassador, who joined with them in advising caution—but the

almost spontaneous impulse of the common folk of
the North let loose the first and last civil war of
Elizabeth's reign.

Over moor and dale echoed the peal of the
church bells rung backwards, the historic call to
arms in those parts. At the sound shepherds and
farmers took up their weapons, pike or harquebus,
and joined the human stream converging on horse
or foot from hill and valley on their various assembly
points. They sang as they marched, songs of piety
and defiance. For uniform they wore on breast or
sleeve a badge depicting the Five Wounds of Christ,
and the standards they followed were the silver
crucifixes and the painted banners also depicting the
Five Wounds, taken from the churches where their
fathers had left them after the failure of the Pilgrimage of Grace thirty-three years before. When
mustered for battle they numbered some 2,500,
chiefly horsemen. Some marched on Durham, where
the restoration of the Catholic faith was proclaimed
with the destruction of the Communion Table and
the Book of Common Prayer, and the Mass celebrated in the cathedral with all its traditional
splendour. Some laid siege to Barnard's Castle, a
royal stronghold, which soon capitulated, others
captured the port of Hartlepool to prepare the way
for the arrival of the troops the Duke of Alba was
expected to send from the Netherlands, still others

pressed on to liberate Mary Stuart, who at the first alarm had been hurried south to Tutbury in Staffordshire.

For a moment it seemed that they might make themselves masters of the whole of the North and be able to treat with the government in such strength as to compel the acceptance of at least part of their demands. There was no royal army near, and Elizabeth's Deputy at York, the Earl of Sussex, dared not call out the militia for fear it would desert to them. But the government possessed one supreme advantage which the rebels lacked, leadership. While their leaders wavered, confused and uncertain between one purpose and another, Elizabeth acted with the energy and determination she seemed always able to summon to the extent that they were needed. As the northern column advanced on Tutbury, they learned that Mary Stuart had already been removed to Coventry, far out of their reach. While their followers gazed across the North Sea for the help from Alba that never came, Elizabeth called up the trained bands from the central and southern counties both to secure the defence of the capital and to proceed to the suppression of the rebellion. In the face of these preparations, and the poor response of those on whom they had counted, the rebel forces fell back and, as the royal troops moved forward, began to disperse to their homes.

The Earls of Northumberland and Westmorland fled and hid themselves among Mary Stuart's sympathisers in Scotland.

As usual with such widespread outbreaks, this one did not die down at once. One of the northern lords, Leonard Dacres, who had refused to join at the beginning because of a quarrel with Norfolk, declined to lay down his arms when the rest did so and to come to Court when Elizabeth summoned him to explain himself. She sent her cousin, Lord Hunsdon, with a small force to bring him in; a battle ensued which Hunsdon won, and Dacres likewise fled for safety over the border. His followers were not so lucky; like those of the two earls, they remained behind to bear the punishment. It fell worst on the poor, for the rich had friends and could buy themselves off; by the time the royal officials had finished, six hundred hung from the gallows as a ghastly warning of the Queen's determination to have the full obedience of her subjects.

Upon the two principal figures in the whole tragic affair the warning was lost. Mary Stuart and Norfolk had both been spared, the Duke even being released from the Tower and restored to the Privy Council on his promise to behave himself thereafter. Many thought that Elizabeth was wrong to have let him off, a great many more that she had been wrong to let off Mary Stuart. Parliament pleaded with her, convinced that so long as the Queen of Scots lived Elizabeth herself and the peace of the realm would never be safe. But Elizabeth could not bring herself to kill the chief of her nobility, believing—and in this most of his opponents among her ministers agreed with her—that Norfolk had learned his lesson and would no longer dabble in plots. Elizabeth still clung to the theory that it would be wrong, a bad example to all subjects, including her own, if she admitted that a Queen could be called to account for her acts by any one other than God. What she wanted was to be safely rid of Mary, preferably by sending her back to Scotland to occupy her own throne or share it with her son, having as her ministers Scots favourable to England who would see that she attempted no mischief towards that country. To secure this Elizabeth tried one way after another, but in vain. Just as she appeared to be reaching a satisfactory compromise, something would happen, such as the assassination of the Earl of Murray, Regent for the baby King and England's chief friend in Scotland; the balance of the parties then shifted against Elizabeth, and something else would have to be tried. And meanwhile Mary, losing patience, again resorted to conspiracy to gain her freedom and again drew the Duke of Norfolk in with her.

This new conspiracy, known as the Ridolfi plot, is too complicated to follow in detail, and turned out in any event to be too hopeless to make it worth while doing so. Ridolfi was a Florentine banker doing business with many important people in London and on the Continent, and therefore a very useful go-between—better than the Spanish Ambassador, who after the troubles in the North had been ordered to leave the country. Ridolfi's plan was to make sure of a Spanish invasion of England to accompany another rising, which would be carefully prepared in advance with the aid of foreign arms and money to be supplied chiefly by the King of Spain and the Pope. The Pope had already issued the long-awaited Bull of Excommunication against Elizabeth, thus giving rebellion the authority which in so many Catholic eyes the previous one had lacked; and a brave man had dared to affix it to the door of St. Paul's Cathedral, and suffered the terrible penalty for his rashness. But that was about all. Ridolfi wrote optimistic letters from abroad to Mary or Norfolk, assuring them that all was going well; they on their side passed on his information to their friends in England and Scotland, and when they could sent them money. Philip II, however, frowned on the whole idea. He disapproved of the Bull of Excommunication being published before there were means of enforcing it, and saw no reason why he should take on the job himself with so much else on his hands; his Governor-general in the Netherlands, the Duke of Alba, declined as before to risk his troops until Mary and Norfolk showed their ability to win and hold a substantial portion of English soil first. And meanwhile Cecil and his secret agents quietly intercepted and read Ridolfi's correspondence before passing it on. When they knew all they wanted to, Mary was suddenly isolated in close captivity and Norfolk returned to the Tower.

Him even Elizabeth could no longer save. Parliament and the country, aroused and frightened by the feeling of secret and constant peril, all but threatened to withdraw their loyal affection if she would not think first of them. In a sense she had to give up Norfolk for Mary, since the country would not have stood again for both being spared : and Mary she still would not surrender to the executioner because of her repugnance to removing a crowned head. So Norfolk went to the block, in June, 1572, while Mary, after another terrific battle over her between Elizabeth and Parliament, continued to brood for nearly fifteen years more on how to turn the tables on the cousin who had so far both defeated and protected her at every encounter.

## * 5 *

## The Middle Years

On November 17th, 1570, the twelfth anniversary of Elizabeth's accession, the one immediately following the suppression of the Northern Rebellion, the bells were rung with unusual fervour; for the day had been set aside as a holiday of national rejoicing, to be celebrated thereafter each year with increasing enthusiasm. Happy to have escaped the horrors of a civil war, and grateful to Elizabeth for having led them through the danger, the English people looked round them and felt their gratitude increase as they saw more and more clearly what she had saved them from. On all sides were strife and bloodshed: in the Low Countries, where the Spaniards and the Dutch struggled to and fro killing and burning; in France, where Catholic and Protestant massacred and looted one another for the control of the State almost without pause; in Scotland, where the factions took turn and turn about doing the same thing on a smaller scale. In England there was at least internal peace, harvests were on the whole good, trade in general flourished, the taxes, owing to England keeping out of war, remained low. There were bad spots in the picture—unemployment in certain industries, want in certain regions, the desolation of those of the old faith to whom the future had begun to look hopeless; but to most the total effect was satisfactory. What was more, it had been obtained not by a passive withdrawal from the world, a fearful desire to be let alone and trouble nobody: never were the English sea-rovers more active, never the hauls they brought home greater. It was in the course of the 1570's that Drake set out upon the first English circumnavigation of the earth with his ship *Pelican*—later renamed *Golden Hind*—to return loaded to danger-point with captured Spanish treasure. The London merchants were allowed to fit out an expedition under Sir Humphrey Gilbert to aid the Dutch when they appeared on the point of exhaustion; an expeditionary force moved swiftly into Scotland to put down England's enemies there when they temporarily seized the government from her friends; while as a precaution against Spain turning to seek revenge, Elizabeth entered into a defensive alliance with the old enemy, France.

Nor was it only their present peace and security that caused Englishmen to rejoice. They had the feeling that under Elizabeth destiny was on their side; that they were approaching a time of glory in their history beyond anything they had known in the past. The feeling arose not only from their material prosperity or the evidences of their success in distant places; it was in the very air. They took fresh survey of their land and institutions and found them good; never before had there been such an outburst of writing about English scenery, artistic monuments and habits of life. But along with the labours of the scholar and the antiquarian—men like Leland, Camden, Stow and others—another and greater kind of writing had already begun to appear: the early poetry of young men dedicated to adventure and the service of the State like Edmund Spenser, Sir Philip Sidney and Sir Walter Raleigh. And hardly would they reach their early prime when the boys still at school—Shakespeare, Bacon, Marlowe and a host of others—would express the same inspiration in an even greater way.

Counting their blessings and their hopes, the English gave the chief credit to their Queen. As well as thanking God for her a great many, rather shockingly, spoke of and to her as if she *were* their god; one of her noblemen, writing to a bishop who dallied in acceding to a wish of hers, referred to her as " our God on earth." In letters addressed and the many works dedicated to her by men of learning and genius, there is distinctly this note of what can only be called worship. And if we try to explain it by calling it flattery, because the writers of the letters and the books wanted something from her, we are up against the fact that they wrote about her the same way after she was dead and beyond granting favours.

But this was only half the story. As well as being a goddess to her people, Elizabeth was also a woman: she knew how to command not only their reverence and gratitude, but their strong personal affection and an admiration by no means untinged with amusement. They liked her to be splendid, to have a brilliant Court, wear gorgeous clothes and talk up to the greatest kings like an equal if not more. They felt themselves sharers in her greatness when from the lofty height of her throne she bade Parliament, like a class of unruly boys, to cease troubling her with their demands and to leave the public welfare to her whose " chief care is always for you," and whose princely concern it was " to keep you from tumbling into the ditch." But they also loved, and retold with relish, the countless stories of her humanity and her unconventionality: how she would notice a humble person in a crowd and invite him to come forward and speak with her; how she would with a kind word relieve a small official charged with addressing her on behalf of his townsfolk and horribly embarrassed by his task; how, having changed her mind three times in one day about going somewhere and overhearing a carter say, " Now I see that the Queen is a woman as well as my wife," she shouted from her window, " What a villain is this! " and ordered some money to be given him to stop his mouth. When amused or displeased she let everybody know it with a " good round oath." Those in her immediate circle she gave pet nicknames to, such as " my Moor " to Walsingham because of his swarthy complexion, or " my monkey " to a Frenchman whose name and character suggested that tricky little animal; yet when Walsingham publicly opposed her on so serious a matter as going to war, she did not hesitate to emphasise her point of view by taking off her slipper and throwing it at him.

She herself was well aware of the two sides of her nature and indeed insisted on them. Her courtiers were expected to address her in words not only suitable to Majesty but as lovers addressed their mistresses. No one was ever allowed to forget that she was the Queen, but her way of calling attention to the fact often amusingly brought out the woman. Once, somewhat later than the point in the story we have reached, a newly arrived Polish Ambassador asked for an audience, which she granted, thinking he came to convey his master's compliments and proposals of friendship. Instead, after the usual

ceremony of kissing her hand, he withdrew a few
paces and began a speech in Latin threatening her
with all manner of unpleasant things. Furious,
Elizabeth stood up and in Latin as fluent as his own
she told him what she thought of him. His king was
a poor sort of creature, a young man reigning by
right of election and not of royal descent; as for
the Ambassador himself—" although I perceive you
have read many books to fortify your arguments,
yet am I apt to believe that you have not lighted
upon the chapter that prescribes the form to be used
towards princes . . ." Her anger was so terrible
that those present were appalled: but Elizabeth,
having had her say, turned with a comic expression
to Cecil and remarked what a pity it was that the
Earl of Essex, her current favourite, then away at
sea, was not present to admire the excellence of
her Latin.

With time her personal peculiarities increased
rather than diminished, and with them her ascendancy over the hearts and minds of her subjects.
Without that popularity, indeed, her reign would
have been quite another thing. Because of it her
statesmen, courtiers, poets and adventurers were
able to make a romance of their services and behave
towards her as if she were an ageless Fairy Princess
and they her adoring swains; not only men who
wanted honour and profit, but high-souled men of

genius and courage like Sir Philip Sidney, whom she
rebuked and punished but who went on adoring
her as his Fairy Princess just the same. The spell
may be said to have spread even to those whom
one would normally have expected to be her
enemies, men like Pope Sixtus V, who exclaimed,
" She certainly is a great Queen and were she only
a Catholic she would be our dearly beloved. . . .
She is only a woman, only mistress of half an island,
and yet she makes herself feared by Spain, by
France, by the Empire, by all! " Even the rebellion
in the North had been directed less against her than
against her ministers, in the hope of persuading her
to change them and their policy. Even the Bull of
Excommunication, which could be read, and by
many was read, as an encouragement to assassinate
her, failed to produce many willing to do so, even
amongst those who would have regarded the deed
as an act of religious virtue. In fact, when her
ministers and the ruling classes in general, frightened
of an attempt at assassination, tried to go beyond the
law and drew up an agreement whereby any one
who made the attempt might be killed at sight
without trial, many of her subjects strongly opposed
to her in matters of policy signed the agreement in
all good faith.

But though England was on the whole prosperous

and hopeful, though by comparison with her neighbours she enjoyed internal peace, she could not evade the fact that the world of which she formed a part was torn by hatred and strife as fierce as any in human history. Men were still far from recognising that two religions could exist side by side in the same society; they believed that the toleration of another religion different from their own, and hence necessarily false, must inevitably destroy such a society and bring the souls of all its members into danger of hell. So the struggle went on with increasing fury within each nation to impose a single creed upon every subject, and within the general society of Christendom to impose it upon every nation. In England the Reformers, or Protestants, aided by the power of the Crown, had at this stage triumphed, but over Europe as a whole Rome was beginning to recover some of the ground it had lost after Martin Luther's revolt in the earlier part of the century. It did this in two ways, by the activities of its missionaries, as in parts of Germany, or by the military might of the Catholic Powers, as in the Low Countries, where the Dutch provinces were sometimes near their last extremity under the pressure of Spanish arms. Against England, the most important of all the Protestant nations to reconquer, military might was not yet possible because the Catholic Powers were too occupied and divided:

and so, in the 1570's, Rome bent her efforts, as she had done a thousand years before in the days of Saint Augustine, to win England back by means of her missionaries.

These were young Englishmen who had either never given up the old faith or, having done so, had returned to it and felt called to become priests. There being, of course, no Catholic seminaries left in England, they went abroad, at first quite easily, later with difficulty and danger, to study in the English colleges at Douai or Rome: the former established for the training of ordinary or secular clergy, the other for the members of the Society of Jesus, commonly known as Jesuits, a new Order established by St. Ignatius Loyola some thirty years before. The seculars came first; they achieved a success which even the most eager could hardly have expected. Cool-minded and well-informed men, like Cecil, had long surmised that the conversion of the English people to Protestantism was far from complete; many—Cecil thought even the majority —had conformed out of fear, self-interest or— possibly the commonest reason of all—sheer bewilderment at the rapid changes in doctrine and forms of worship imposed on them in so short a time. Thus it happened that the missionaries found a welcome, not only with the families who had secretly offered them hospitality if they came, but with many others whom their first hosts invited to meet them or passed them on to. They would land at the ports in disguise, as merchants, courtiers or what not, professing some plausible business in the country, and make by devious ways for their first house of refuge. There they would administer the Sacraments and preach to the households and to such of the neighbours as their hosts trusted, and presently go on to some other locality to which they were directed or received a call: always in disguise, vestments and sacred vessels often dangerously concealed about their persons, passing the long hours when they were not actively engaged in their priestly duties hiding in some walled-up portion of a country house or, if the chase got too hot, in a wood. Not a few old manor-houses still possess their " priests' holes," artfully contrived by the Elizabethan owner to defeat the searches of the royal pursuivants.

The activities, the cunning and the cruelty of these man-hunters increased in proportion as the missionaries became more numerous and successful. The ruling classes, and the Protestants in general, grew frightened to the point of panic. If England were reconverted to Catholicism, their religion and their ascendancy in the State would be overthrown, the property and the livelihood of many of them brought into jeopardy. They did not believe that the priests had come only to convert; they thought that the

Bull of Excommunication had been intended to encourage the assassination of Queen Elizabeth so that a Catholic successor—most probably Mary Stuart—could be put in her place, and that the priests were sent to carry out this sinister design. As fast as they could be tracked down they were, therefore, put on trial for high treason, a process carrying with it the dreadful penalty of being hanged, then cut down and disembowelled while still alive. They might, as the law stood, have been tried on purely religious grounds, for saying Mass and inducing others to hear it; but the English people, though far from tolerant, would have had little sympathy with this kind of persecution, particularly after their experience under Mary, and the government deemed it more prudent to punish the priests as traitors and spies bent on the subverting of the State rather than as apostles of a forbidden creed.

That they were actually traitors, with a papal commission to murder Elizabeth, few historians now believe; their last audible words were commonly a prayer for her and the prosperity of her realm. Nor did she herself, although she consented to their deaths, apparently regard them as traitors and assassins. One, the most famous, Edmund Campion, the Jesuit, she had befriended when he was a brilliant young scholar at Oxford, and after his capture had private speech with him; others she is reported to have helped to escape abroad from her own officers. But even she could not have protected them after they were caught since she had strained her prerogative of mercy to the utmost in sparing the Queen of Scots. Had she also spared the missionaries, Parliament, her ministers and other chief subjects would have regarded her as so idiotically indifferent to their and her safety as to be scarcely fit to rule.

Indeed, many of those who admired her most and served her best increasingly felt that she quite underestimated the dangers confronting her, and the means necessary to overcome them. Despite her help to the Dutch, the Spaniards were by the late 1570's reconquering them bit by bit. Elsewhere, too, the Protestant cause appeared to be in decline, the extreme Catholic faction, headed by Mary Stuart's relatives the Guises, all but triumphant in France, large tracts of Germany, the original centre of Protestantism, reconverted by the efforts of the Jesuit missionaries. The critics of Elizabeth's policy held that the small and underhanded aid given to the Dutch leader William of Orange, even with the injuries inflicted on Spanish trade by the English sea-rovers, would no longer do: that if Spain succeeded in finally subduing the Netherlands, she would turn her might, perhaps in conjunction with the other Catholic powers, to the conquest of England; and that the only way for England to avert the peril was to join the Dutch in a full-scale war and throw the Spaniards out of the Netherlands once and for all.

Of the men who thought this way the most prominent was the Earl of Leicester, still Elizabeth's favourite though he had begun to lose his looks, who had finally taken up his position with the extreme or Puritan wing of the Protestants. But the ablest of them was Sir Francis Walsingham, now Principal Secretary—Cecil having become Lord Treasurer and a peer under the title of Lord Burghley —who amongst his other duties looked after the realm's internal security and in that capacity kept watch on the missionaries and upon the many complicated plots centring on Mary Stuart. Round Leicester and Walsingham soon gathered some of the most remarkable of the younger Elizabethans, including Sir Walter Raleigh—a Devonian like Drake, Hawkins and Sir Humphrey Gilbert—and Philip Sidney, Leicester's nephew and Walsingham's son-in-law.

Elizabeth used and rewarded them but refused to hearken to them. War, as she repeatedly told them, she hated with every instinct of her being. Its glories, for the sake of which her father had all but bankrupted his kingdom, meant nothing to her comparable with its uncertainties and waste. Moreover, she did not agree with the purposes of the war that Leicester and Walsingham were urging her to. As in the case of the Scots and Mary Stuart she did not like to be in the position of supporting rebels against their lawful sovereign: the precedent might well be used against other sovereigns, including herself. If circumstances required her to give help to the Dutch, as formerly to the Scots, for her own and England's preservation, she would do so, but to the smallest extent necessary. Rebellion and revolution for their own sake she was not prepared to finance. Nor had she any interest in the Protestant cause as such. Her religious feelings were not strong in either direction, and she could be as happy with Catholic as with Protestant fellow-kings—happier even, since the former as a rule had an older and grander tradition of royalty—so long as they let her and her people alone.

Nevertheless she could not but admit that in one all-important respect the war party was right: that if the Netherlands went under, England might well follow. Philip II would not only have the means—the finest army in the world freed for other action should the Dutch collapse—but the motive: a motive immensely reinforced by Drake's voyage round the world in 1577-80, in the course of which he took so much Spanish treasure that he had to throw mere silver overboard to lighten his vessel and was able on his return to repay the investors in the voyage, chief amongst them the Queen, forty-seven times their original stake. Since Elizabeth could not afford to allow the Netherlands to be reconquered and yet was unwilling to go to war to defend them, she had to think of some other way. The way she thought of was characteristic, a woman's rather than a warrior's. It involved getting a man to do her fighting for her.

The man she selected was Francis, Duke of Anjou, brother of King Henry III of France. (Charles IX had died in 1577.) Anjou was ambitious and had nothing much to do. His brother the King regarded him as a nuisance and was anxious to be rid of him on almost any terms. It was Elizabeth's idea that he should become her fiancé—he had already been her suitor for years, though something like a quarter of a century younger than she—and with financial help from his brother and herself raise an army in France with which to carve a kingdom for himself out of the Spanish Netherlands. Thus she would be rid of the menace of Spain and at the same time avert a danger equally great, that France itself, another mighty military power, would establish itself in Spain's place. For Anjou, apart from being her husband and owing her money, would be too jealous of his royal brother to be likely to hold his kingdom at the disposal of France.

Though Anjou took to the idea as strongly as did

Elizabeth, there were various difficulties in the way of carrying it out. On the part of Henry III there was the fear that Elizabeth would not, or would insufficiently, make good her part of the bargain, thus throwing the responsibility for his brother's doings on him and involving him in a quarrel with Spain. On the part of the Netherlands there was a natural objection to being made the pawn of other people's ambitions and a considerable doubt of the value of exchanging a French master for the Spanish one; they wanted all the help they could get while giving as little for it as possible. But the most difficult problem was Anjou himself. Elizabeth hoped that he would be satisfied with a certain amount of money in advance and her promise to marry him when he had defeated her enemies for her; Anjou preferred that she should marry him first, fearing that otherwise she might leave him in the lurch after he *had* engaged her enemies for her. It was too big a risk for her to take, so she invited him to visit her in the hope that her words would sound more persuasive face to face than by letter.

He came: an ugly little man with a pock-marked face, a huge bulbous nose and a beard so wispy that even his mother apologised for it. But Elizabeth was not put off; far from it. She made it plain that she considered him an unusually attractive young man and nicknamed him her little Frog on the spot. She may not have meant to marry him, but she certainly acted as if she did, and took in not only many observers but quite possibly herself. Sir Philip Sidney was banished from Court for speaking, and a preacher named Stubbs had his right hand cut off for preaching against the marriage; even her darling Leicester received a scolding for opposing it. She went so far as to promise her suitor in public that she would definitely marry him, and sealed her promise—as it must have seemed to all—with a kiss. Perhaps she was not entirely insincere. That she wanted to make use of Anjou in her country's interest is beyond doubt, but she was getting on for fifty now and may well have wondered whether she had, after all, been wise in giving up a normal woman's life in marriage. Perhaps the discovery that Leicester had deceived her by secretly marrying a distant cousin of hers may have had something to do with her feelings: and it may not be without significance that the opposition on the part of certain of her councillors to Anjou is one of the rare instances when she was openly seen to weep.

At any rate, Anjou seems to have believed her and went off to the Netherlands with her ring on his finger and her money in his coffers. But he proved a sad disappointment. For he failed to beat the enemy or to win the affections of the people whose king he hoped to be. Presently he returned to Elizabeth for a renewal of her promise and still more money. He received both, and great honours as well, but this time Elizabeth sent him away in somewhat unloverly haste and on his return to the Low Countries he failed as dismally as before. Discouraged, he returned to France to die of the tubercular ailment that had already carried off so many of his brothers and sisters. Very soon after, in July, 1584, the man who from the beginning had been the heart and soul of Dutch resistance, William of Orange, died also, at the hands of an assassin: and Elizabeth was at last confronted with the grim knowledge that unless she actively took up his cause, it might well be lost and England with it.

# * 6 *

## The Test

THE SUPREME crisis of Elizabeth's reign was now upon her. For nearly thirty years she had been trying to avoid it, and though her people chiefly remember her for the greatness with which she met it, her best claim to greatness as a stateswoman was in putting it off until she could meet it with a real chance of success. Almost from the day she was born there had been the danger that the Powers of Europe would combine in arms to compel England's return to the Roman obedience. Elizabeth herself, coming to the throne as a Protestant ruler bound to terminate the temporary reconciliation with the papacy under her predecessor, had found England's historic enemies, the French, established on her only land frontier, in Scotland, and driven them out. Yet she managed to make friends of them and keep them from helping Mary Stuart. With Mary in her power she had managed on the whole to maintain a friendly government in Scotland and overcome

Mary's threat to the internal peace of England. And all the while she had kept in check the might of Spain, on land in the Low Countries and by sea everywhere. One enemy had been isolated from another until the principal enemy stood virtually isolated, much of his strength drained from him by rebellion and the assaults of the English seamen upon the sources of his power. However little one may approve of Elizabeth's methods, they averted the combination—the Great Enterprise, as her contemporaries called it—which would have destroyed her. Had she failed to avert it England might well have been invaded and reduced to dependency on her conquerors: a condition little likely to favour an Age of Shakespeare or the founding of an empire overseas.

This was her true achievement. It was for others to make England great and splendid and spiritually worthy. Hers as ruler was to keep their island home secure so that their genius and energy might range in freedom. They could attempt the heroic precisely because she, in her conduct of their affairs, avoided heroics, preferring to rely upon prudence, caution and common sense. Yet in one important respect she could claim to be a sharer with them: she was able to personify for them the England they loved in common, make it possible for them to believe they were serving it, a thing, by serving her, a person.

Even war did not alter her; for better and worse she remained herself. She regarded it not as a glorious drama affording her an incomparable opportunity to play the heroine, but as a grim and unpleasant necessity to be got over in the shortest time and with the smallest risk and expense possible. Her poets might compare her with Minerva, her artists paint her as Bellona in shining helmet on a prancing horse, but only once, on one supreme occasion, did she appear before her people in any such martial guise. To the delegates of the seven Provinces still in rebellion, when they came over to solicit her help, she showed herself a shrewd, hard bargainer, mindful above all of her country's interests. In return for her help they offered her sovereignty over them. It was a temptation few princes could have resisted, but she refused the offer, to the regret of many of her leading subjects, because she did not want to commit England to an endless war by annexing another king's dominions. The help she could not refuse, because the Provinces' need was also hers. But she gave it in limited quantities on strict terms, which required the Dutch to repay her, after peace was made, whatever she spent on the army she was to equip and send, and meantime to hand over several of their principal seaports in pledge until the debt was paid.

Late in 1585 her expeditionary force set out under

the command of the Earl of Leicester. He was not
an ideal commander, having had no experience of
war since his youth, and being by temperament
haughty and with little regard for the feelings of
others. But he was her most conspicuous subject,
made so by her favour, and the most influential
advocate of the policy which had led to his country's
intervention. Moreover, the Dutch expressly asked
for him in the belief that Elizabeth's partiality for
him would cause her to support him better than any
other general.

In this they proved to be mistaken. Leicester
found the Provinces not only on the verge of defeat
but of internal anarchy. Their troops were irregularly paid, hungry, ragged and mutinous. Some of
the money sent over to pay her own troops had to
be diverted to them. But the English troops themselves were soon in nearly the same state, aggravated
for them by the unfamiliar severity of the Dutch
winter. Corruption had always been common in
armies; the companies were raised by their captains,
who managed to draw pay for more men than they
had, sometimes by borrowing men from other captains
to answer at musters, and otherwise to divert the
Queen's money into their own pockets. One can
see how the system worked in the wonderful scene
of Falstaff recruiting his troops in *Henry IV, Part 1*.
Discontent grew on both sides. In the hope of

overcoming it and so prosecuting the war with greater success, the Dutch offered Leicester the governorship of the Provinces, an office making him their civil and military chieftain and virtually viceroy for Elizabeth.

Leicester accepted, partly for the reasons that caused the Dutch to offer him the post, partly out of vanity and pride. When Elizabeth heard of what he had done she was beside herself with rage. A creature of hers to do what she herself had refused to do, accept rule over the Netherlands and with it responsibility for them! Proclaim her a liar and cheat before the world which had heard her solemnly declare that she would do no such thing! All this she wrote to Leicester and a good deal more, ordering him immediately and publicly to lay down his office. He answered imploring her to realise that if he did so the Dutch would think she meant to abandon them and might in consequence give up the struggle. There was good sense in this, and her principal ministers, including the old sage Burghley himself, added their voice to his. For a while Elizabeth resisted them; her anger was not lessened when she heard rumours that Leicester's wife, whom she detested, was fitting herself out to go to The Hague with the state of a queen. But good sense prevailed and she allowed Leicester to continue in his governorship until he could without harm to the common cause resign it. Meantime she did, in fact, to help out her needy soldiers, send more money than she had promised to do.

She had her own ideas of the kind of war she meant to fight, and to what extent, and meant to carry them through. But wars cannot be fought, as has often been remarked, upon a principle of limited liability. She may have been wrong to try to do it this way. Unluckily her resources did not permit her to do it any other way. And the results were not encouraging. The English and Dutch in 1586 suffered defeat after defeat at the hands of the incomparable Spanish infantry under their great general the Prince of Parma, Philip II's nephew. Only one battle lightened the gloomy picture, the skirmish at Zutphen, near Arnhem—a brilliant, aimless affair straight out of the pages of chivalry, in which Leicester himself fought hand to hand and his nephew, Sir Philip Sidney, received his death-wound and with the immortal words, " Thy need is greater than mine," passed the drink offered him over to the poor soldier dying of thirst.

While the English troops fought and starved in the Netherlands, unsuccessfully but not vainly, since they were helping to keep Dutch resistance alive, other and possibly greater dangers were threatening at home. The obvious way for Elizabeth's enemies to stop her interference with their affairs was to invade England, and this they had long meditated off and on. But invasion was a slow, costly and hazardous business; assassination, if it could be brought about, would be quicker, safer and cheaper, and as Elizabeth's activity abroad increased, her enemies concentrated more and more upon the possibility of getting rid of her and the whole existing regime in England by one murderous stroke. Several plots for that purpose had been uncovered in recent years, too obscure, complicated or unimportant to describe in detail. Their effect had been to alarm the English people to the point of panic. They did not doubt that these plots had been hatched in the interests of Mary Stuart, to make her Queen by removing Elizabeth. If Elizabeth were in fact assassinated, the Privy Council and the Courts of Justice would cease to function, since the members held their commissions from her; with the government and the judicial system temporarily suspended, Mary Stuart would be able to step into the vacancy, appoint her own officials, pardon the murderers and punish her opponents. To avert this disaster a Bond of Association was drawn up and signed by thousands of leading Englishmen, pledging that if Elizabeth were assassinated, the person in whose interest the deed was done should not only not succeed but might be killed by any one as an outlaw on sight.

This was, however, a little too primitive a method of justice even for many who approved the general purpose of the Bond, and when it came before Parliament to be enacted into law, it was amended so as to allow an offender the benefit of trial before a Special Commission provided for in the Act. It was under this law that Mary Stuart was now to pay with her life for the most serious and dramatic attempt yet devised upon Elizabeth's.

It is known in history as the Babington Conspiracy, from the name of the young man who became its most prominent member, though he did not originate it. That is supposed to have been done by a priest named John Ballard, whose part in the affair was as mysterious as in other matters with which he was associated; to this day it is not certain which side he was on, whether Elizabeth's or her enemies' or both. But this was a characteristic of many plotters of the time, who could not make up their minds where their loyalty lay and were prepared to take pay simultaneously from Walsingham, the head of the Queen's secret service, and from his formidable adversary the Spanish ambassador or other foreign sources. This of course added to the difficulty of protecting Elizabeth, who made matters worse for her protectors by poohpoohing their fears and apparently never having any of her own. In this instance the difficulty was especially great because of the fact that Babington, a young man of good family, enlisted a number of others with positions at Court whom there was no reason to suspect. Of these, six were to kill Elizabeth at the moment that the foreign invasion and internal rising promised by Ballard to Babington was signalled; the rest of the band was to make for Chartley in Staffordshire, where Mary was then in captivity, overpower her guards and bring her back as Queen.

It might have happened so, at least the part referring to Elizabeth's death, had not her servants been sleeplessly vigilant and had not luck come to the aid of their cunning. Ever since her removal to Chartley, at the end of 1585, Mary had been in touch with the outside world by means of a brewer in nearby Burton from whom she bought the beer for her household. In the full casks sent to Chartley he hid the letters for her from her correspondents, in the empty ones returned to Burton he smuggled out hers to them. Thus she thought that she had a secure channel for receiving reports from and issuing her orders to her agents in England, Scotland and on the Continent. What she did not know until it was too late was that the man through whom the arrangement with the brewer was made was in Walsingham's pay, as was the brewer himself; and that her letters were decoded and read by Walsingham's extremely able assistants before being passed on to their destinations. In answer to a harmless letter from her to Babington, a former page and admirer of hers, he wrote describing for her the plot against Elizabeth. These the Queen's sleuths read and waited for what Mary would say in return. They did not wait in vain; in her reply she warmly approved of the plot and made various suggestions with regard to it. This letter Walsingham also had copied and passed on, adding to it a forged passage requesting Babington to send Mary the list of his fellow-conspirators who had been designated for the killing of Elizabeth.

The list was never sent, for before Babington got round to it the authorities became alarmed lest the plot be put into execution while they waited for their evidence and decided to round up the conspirators on the evidence they already had. Mary's belongings were ransacked while she was out hunting, her two secretaries arrested and she herself moved to close captivity nearby. Amidst the wild rejoicing of the populace, expressed in songs, bonfires and the ringing of bells, Babington and his accomplices were led to the Tower, whence shortly they were brought out to die seven at a time on two successive days— a spectacle so horrible that Elizabeth let the second batch off the full torments prescribed by the law. But the rejoicings were nevertheless tempered by a great fear, the fear that Elizabeth would again let the Queen of Scots off and leave England in as great a danger of insurrection and invasion as before.

It was no time for half-measures. Though war was as yet undeclared, England was engaged in one as desperate as any in her history. Men could simply not believe that the two systems, Catholic and Protestant, were capable of existing side by side in the same universe; to those who regarded one of these creeds as true, as the secret of the good life in this world and salvation in the next, the other signified earthly ruin and eternal damnation. To the English people Elizabeth and Mary stood as the symbols and supports of these irreconcilable creeds. Their love of the one was as immoderate, as fanatical, as their hatred of the other: if one were to remain alive, the other simply had to be dead. So if Elizabeth, who had the power of decision, were now to spare Mary, she would in the eyes of her admirers be guilty of a great wrong to herself, to them, to England, to God; would in a sense be collaborating with the enemy and deserving of the same fate. The very love that caused people to want her to destroy Mary might well turn to hate if she refused to do so.

Elizabeth, of course, knew all this. The decision was the most difficult of her life, and for almost the only time in her life it brought her to a state something like hysteria. That for her own safety and

England's Mary ought to die she did not doubt, but she did not want the responsibility of causing her death. Mary was not only her cousin, her next-of-kin, but a Queen like herself, who had sought and received her hospitality in need. She was terrified of her own conscience, of God Who had never made one queen judge of another; she was if anything more terrified of what her peers, the princes of Europe, would say if she treated her royal captive so.

But there were the grim men round her pressing her to remember what she owed to them who had so long and loyally served her, and to the people of England who looked to her to defend them in this time of mortal danger. She was, after all, Sovereign under the law, and had herself signed the law which defined Mary's offence and prescribed the penalty. . . . She could not do other than let the law take its course. A Commission of lords, ministers and judges proceeded to Fotheringay in Northampton-shire, where Mary, though denying their right to try her, nevertheless appeared before them and defended herself with a majesty which emphasised the brutal one-sidedness of the proceedings and rendered it difficult for posterity to review impartially the real strength of the evidence against her. Before the commissioners could render their verdict, Elizabeth again changed her mind and sent them a message forbidding them to do so. Again her ministers, back from Fotheringay, argued with her, and again she could not resist, and allowed the Commission to bring in a verdict which judged Mary to have forfeited her life.

But sentence was not execution . . . and only Elizabeth's signature on the death warrant could cause Mary's head to fall. Lords and Commons unanimously petitioned Elizabeth to sign. In a scene so moving that nearly all present wept, she begged them not to press her—swore that she had their interests always before her—but that she would not, could not; at least not yet. She hoped some way might be found . . . perhaps Mary would repent and alter . . . or some good security for her conduct in the future be found. But all this, to Parliament and her ministers, perhaps inwardly to herself, was mere words. Wild rumours broke out—of Mary's escape, a Spanish invasion, a new attempt on Elizabeth's life; some of them perhaps spread by the men round her who were trying to bring her to a resolution. At last they succeeded to the extent of persuading her to sign the warrant.

But even then she refused to send it. She was still hoping for something that would spare her the terrible responsibility. Often alone, in tears, her nerves in tatters, she allowed herself to imagine a way out so horrible that to us it seems almost insane in its desperation. If someone were quietly to assassinate Mary, the same end would be served without her having to bear the blame. She had the suggestion put to Mary's keeper, Sir Amyas Paulet, a stiff, upright Puritan who repudiated it in disgust. She was angry with him, but not too angry, for she saw his point of view even if she—and many others in that age—did not share it. Her ministers finally settled the question by sending the warrant off on their own. On the morning of February 8th, 1587, just twenty years less a day after Darnley's murder, Mary was executed in the Great Hall of Fotheringay. In a fearful revulsion Elizabeth placed the blame for dispatching the warrant on her junior secretary, William Davison, and had him confined for a while in the Tower. This unjust act at least enabled her to explain to her critics amongst her fellow-monarchs that the final responsibility had not been hers.

If they did not entirely believe her, the story was plausible enough to prevent them from blaming her too severely. In England itself little blame was felt, only a great relief, and the effect from a practical point of view was good. For now those who detested Elizabeth had nowhere else to turn. Rebellion was useless since, even if it were successful, there was no longer any one to put in her place. And this helped as much as anything to keep the discontented quiet, even loyal, during the tremendous crisis now looming.

For Philip of Spain had at last made up his mind
to strike with all the force he could muster. While
hoping that the Babington plot might save him the
trouble, he had never really counted on its succeeding. Patiently, cautiously, as was his way, he had
set about building a great navy, borrowing for the
purpose where he could, mostly his Italian bankers
and the Pope, Sixtus V. The latter, a shrewd, witty
old man, was, unlike most Europeans, sceptical of
Spain's power to beat England at sea: he openly
admired Elizabeth a good deal more than he did
Philip II, but as Pope could hardly withhold his
support from a Catholic King endeavouring to
subdue a troublesome heretic and disturber of the
peace. By the time of Mary Stuart's death Philip's
navy, already popularly known as the Invincible
Armada, was assembling in the principal ports of
Spain and Portugal, which country Spain had
annexed a few years before. By spring it was
expected to sail for the conquest of England: when
suddenly Elizabeth loosed Drake upon it like a
crashing thunderbolt. With his small squadron he
forced his way into Cadiz Harbour under the guns
of the land defences—guns actually outranged by
those of the new-style English warships which
Hawkins, as Treasurer of the Navy, had for years
been bringing to perfection—blasted the Spanish
ships and burned their accumulated stores. Then

he went on to do the same at Lisbon, and though there the defences proved too strong to force, his demonstration, and his seizure of a nearby base, prevented the fleet within from moving out or being reinforced. On his way home from this magnificent exploit he picked up an East Indian merchantman whose cargo proved to be worth nearly three-fourths of what the defence against the Armada cost.

Philip persisted. He worked and prayed, and his people worked and prayed with him. But fortune seemed increasingly to favour the work and prayers of his enemies. His admiral, the greatest sailor he possessed, died and his place had to be filled by a man who frankly did not believe himself up to the task. When the refurbished Armada set sail in May, 1588, the weather dispersed it and it had to return to re-form, thus giving Elizabeth who, to save expense, had laid up her fleet during the winter, additional time to assemble and re-fit it. For her haste to lay up the fleet, and her extreme thrift in ordering supplies for it, many of her statesmen and admirals then, as well as many historians since, have severely criticised her, but she did not, in fact, know where to turn for money, the English financial system having no provision for hostilities on such a scale. As it was, expenditure began to soar to six times the normal revenue, and had it not been for the 120 ships supplied by the merchants of the seaport towns—two-thirds of the whole—the Royal Navy would have been utterly inadequate to meet the invasion. She was also blamed for not releasing Drake again to operate against the Spanish coasts because she was negotiating with the Spanish commander in the Netherlands for possible terms of peace; but it must be remembered that she never regarded the war in the Netherlands as a fight to a finish, indeed from England's point of view as a war at all, but merely as a means of keeping Spain at a distance, and if this could be secured she was at all times more than anxious to stop the fighting. The test would be how she conducted herself when this policy failed, and to this the answer was now to be given.

In fact she was about to launch another attack on the Armada at its base when word was received, on July 19th, that it had been sighted at the mouth of the Channel. Its object was to sail down-Channel through the Straits of Dover, make contact with Parma on the coast of Belgium and transfer his army across the North Sea for the invasion. This strategy was, of course, unknown to the defenders, and they had therefore to make ready at all points. Defences against a landing were prepared along the South Coast and an army mustered under the veteran soldier, Sir John Norris, " the chicken of Mars," as the Queen called him. Other defences were erected along the East Coast and an army assembled under the Earl of Leicester with headquarters at Tilbury near the mouth of the Thames. For the interception of the Armada at sea the bulk of the fleet was stationed at Plymouth under Sir Francis Drake, with a second squadron under Sir Thomas Howard posted to watch the Straits of Dover should the Spaniards slip past him; over both was the Lord High Admiral, Howard of Effingham.

Drake was nearly caught in Plymouth Harbour by an unfavourable wind, but managed to warp his ships out in time. His tactics were to meet the Armada—ships larger and rather more numerous than his own—in a running fight which would keep them away from the English coast and, taking advantage of the superior sailing qualities and gun-power of his own ships, destroy them piecemeal— " pluck their feathers," in Drake's words—or damage them to the greatest possible extent. In this he succeeded: after a week of it, at an average speed of barely a mile an hour due to the varying winds, the Spanish Admiral tried to break off the fight and take shelter in Calais Roads. But from there the English ousted them by sending in " fireships," vessels loaded with pitch and set alight, so that he was forced to cut cables and make for the open sea. And there a terrible gale caught him, sending many of his ships on to the sandbanks of the Netherlands and driving the rest irresistibly northwards, round Scotland and Ireland, shipwreck following shipwreck, until only a poor battered remnant ever reached a home port again.[1]

So England was saved from the greatest peril she had ever known or would know again for centuries. The rejoicings, following the long-drawn agony of suspense, were something that no one living would ever forget . . . their impression remains stamped for ever upon the literature soon to follow from the generation of young men, many of whom took part in the fighting and the triumph. The climax came with the Queen's ride in her painted chariot, through streets draped with blue cloth and lined with " the Companies of the City standing on both sides with their banners in goodly order," to the Thanksgiving service in St. Paul's Cathedral, hung for the occasion with flags from the wrecked and captured galleons of the Armada. But most unforgettable of all was Elizabeth's conduct throughout those weeks . . . in particular her journey to Tilbury to review her troops and thank them in the wonderful speech which has become part of the treasure of the English language:

" . . . Let tyrants fear. I have always so

---

[1] The full story of the immortal battle will be found in another volume of this series, *Sir Francis Drake*, by J. A. Williamson.

behaved myself that, under God, I have placed my chiefest strength and safeguard in the loyal hearts and good-will of my subjects; and therefore I have come amongst you, as you see, at this time, not for my recreation and disport, but being resolved in the midst and heat of the battle, to live or die amongst you all, to lay down for my God, and for my kingdom, and for my people, my honour and my blood, even in the dust. I know I have the body of a weak and feeble woman, but I have the heart and stomach of a King, and of a King of England, too, and I think foul scorn that Parma, or Spain, or any prince of Europe should dare to invade the borders of my realm. . ."

She had worried people, frightened them, even at times disgusted them with her caution and parsimony, her tricks and dodges, until the crisis was upon her. But when it came she rose to it, made it the supreme occasion of her life in a way that assured her memory so long as England endured.

# * 7 *
## The Last Years

THE YEARS following the victory over the Armada were the most brilliant of Elizabeth's reign, in many respects the most brilliant in English history, indeed in all history; the years in which Marlowe, Shakespeare, Byrd, Spenser, Bacon and so many others caught and enriched the imaginations of their own and all succeeding generations with their poetry, music and wisdom. They were the years also in which English enterprise, spreading far and wide, caused men bearing the Queen's credentials to penetrate to the piratical strongholds of the Barbary Coast, the Sultan's Court at Istanbul and even beyond to half-legendary Persia.

For Elizabeth personally, however, those years were neither so brilliant nor so happy as the thirty that had preceded them. For one thing she was growing old. Though only fifty-five that autumn of 1588, and in comparatively good health, she was already the same age as her father, older by two years than her grandfather and by a good deal than her brother and sister had been when they died; it was not a Tudor characteristic to live long. The men on whose aid and counsel she had depended were going rapidly: Leicester, her best-beloved, died the month after the defeat of the Armada, Walsingham in 1590, Hatton, her Lord Chancellor and second favourite, soon afterwards; only Burghley, thirteen years her senior, lived on until near the end of her reign, but growing frail and glad to hand over an increasing number of his responsibilities to his son.

The younger generation proved harder to manage. Men like Sir Walter Raleigh, soldier, sailor, explorer, poet; Burghley's son Robert, a quiet little hunchback of almost diabolical cleverness; the young Earl of Essex, Leicester's stepson—men like these, though in many ways more gifted and versatile than their predecessors, were, perhaps for that very reason, prone to tear the Court into bitter, unforgiving factions in pursuit of their own particular ends. And despite the remarkable abilities of the men who frequented it, the Court itself was felt to have grown somehow less magnificent, a shade more vulgar, not quite so good a reflection of England's best.

The issues and problems confronting the Queen and her people were likewise changing. Spain still loomed formidable and dangerous, her King meditating other and greater Armadas; but the undeclared war, so long in coming, was slowly shaping, despite occasional resounding exploits by land and sea, towards the undeclared peace that would set in by Elizabeth's death. The Catholics, most of whom had remained loyal during the threatened invasion, were no longer the principal menace to internal tranquillity. That place was being taken by the extreme Protestant sect known as the Puritans, who desired the abolition of bishops and a radical overhaul of the Church's teaching; to them would fall the victory a generation later when they would succeed, at least temporarily, in over-throwing the monarchy itself. Moreover the merchant classes, so long Elizabeth's most enthusi-astic supporters, were no longer content with things as they had been. A great deal of English trade, during this period of expansion, had been carried on under a system of monopolies: a favoured courtier or other highly-placed person being given the exclusive right to import or export certain types of goods—wines or manufactured cloths, for example —and passing this right on to a group of merchants in consideration of a share in the profits. Now a great many other merchants were clamouring to participate in these privileges and demanding that the system of monopolies be ended or drastically modified. The criticism was in itself an indication, one of many, of the movement away from the feudal outlook of the past towards the capitalistic outlook of the century to come. One age was slowly dissolving into another.

Only Elizabeth herself appeared to resist the process of change. True, her red hair was more glaringly false, her cheeks more rouged, her teeth deeply discoloured, the fine pale skin of her face and hands wrinkled and spotted with age. But even physically she had not lost all the vigour of her youth, being still able when she chose to ride half the day and dance half the night. And mentally and spiritually she had scarcely altered at all. Her wit was, if anything, sharper than ever; fun could still warm or displeasure freeze the light blue directness of her gaze; her autocrat's temper, her determination to rule, was as fierce as ever. Nor was her popularity, or her love of it, at all diminished. On the contrary, it had on the whole increased, for it now rested upon solid achievement rather than mere expectation. In the beginning she had been an almost unknown quantity, to whom the people looked to remedy the errors and disasters of her predecessor and somehow bring about a change for the better. In that they, or the majority of them, felt that she had succeeded; they were proud of the dangers and glories through which she had led them; but they now cherished her not as a symbol of the changes they desired, but as their rock of stability, their one sure protection against either reaction or revolutionary experiment. Most of them could by now scarcely remember when she had not been, or imagine her not being, their Queen. For some she had in a sense almost taken the place of God—someone abiding, all-powerful, upon whose love and wisdom the well-being of their world depended.

Not all of her subjects, of course, shared this view, even amongst those most devoted to her service. Some thought that age was making her timorous: that she was not prosecuting the war with enough energy, was trying too hard for peace with Spain, was not sufficiently supporting her ally, the new Huguenot King of France, Henry IV, who was having to fight a war with the extreme Catholics amongst his subjects for his throne. This was not a new criticism: something very like it had been put forward by Leicester, Walsingham and others before she agreed to intervene in the Netherlands, and it was now made by their successors in the leadership of the Puritan faction, of whom the most noteworthy was Sir Walter Raleigh. There were others, how-ever, who while not opposing the war as the Catholic party had done, indeed even urging and taking active part in it, felt critical of Elizabeth on different grounds. They considered that, in the great altera-tion made in the structure of the State under her, she had allowed herself to be led in a seriously wrong direction. Too great power had been concentrated in the Crown at the expense of the old nobility; that power had been subtly grasped by the new race of politicians she had put in charge of her affairs; in short, she had allowed herself to become the tools of the Cecils and their kind, who were using her to increase their own wealth and importance. By far the most prominent of the people who held this sort of opinion was the Earl of Essex.

If ever a man could be called the darling of the gods it was Robert Devereux, Earl of Essex. Pretty nearly everything a man could want he had until—like other darlings of the gods—he wanted too much. In almost every respect he was the ideal of his generation. What it looked for was what the Greeks had looked for, the all-round man—strong and handsome in body, magnanimous of spirit, responsive to beauty and the things of the mind. Essex was fair, tall and beautifully proportioned, a notable athlete and a warrior out of the pages of chivalry. As well as being a lover and patron of the arts, he wrote poems himself of which at least one has been deemed worthy to survive in the anthologies. But what most endeared him to his contemporaries was an openness, a liberality, a sense of honour and truthfulness very rare amongst the aspiring courtiers of the time. Indeed, he was the only one of Elizabeth's favourites ever to be popular: as beloved by the multitude as Leicester, Hatton and Raleigh were detested. Faults he had, and they were to bring about his downfall, but they were never faults of smallness or meanness . . . " one that could not conceal himself but carried his love and his hatred always in his brow." And with it all he had charm capable of turning the head of pretty nearly every one he met of either sex, and to cause men to follow him, even to their doom, against their better judgment. Shakespeare's lines about Hamlet have often been applied to him:

*The courtier's, soldier's, scholar's eye, tongue, sword,*
*The expectancy and rose of the fair state,*
*The glass of fashion and the mould of form,*
*The observed of all observers.*

It is not improbable that Shakespeare had Essex at least partly in mind, for the latter was very much in the public eye when *Hamlet* was written. Moreover, there are other links between the splendid young lord and the king of dramatic poets. Essex's friend and follower, the Earl of Southampton, was Shakespeare's friend and patron; and at the crisis of his fortunes Essex's familiars paid for a public performance of *Richard II* as a kind of prelude to the act of violence against their sovereign which they, like Bolingbroke in the play, were preparing.

His charm worked on Elizabeth as much as on any one. So much so, in fact, as to cause scandalous gossip in certain quarters, especially after their relations developed to the point that

> " When she is abroad, nobody near her but my Lord of Essex; and at night my Lord is at cards, or one game or another with her, that he cometh not to his own lodging till birds sing in the morning . . ."

But such gossip was based on jealousy or misunderstanding. To us it may seem odd that a woman of fifty-four should be receiving love-letters and adoring compliments from a young man of twenty —their respective ages when he took his place at Court. But Elizabeth was not the only sovereign to receive, nor Essex the only courtier to pay such addresses. They were the fashion, though it cannot be denied that she thoroughly enjoyed, nay insisted on, receiving them. The idea of husbands or lovers in any real sense she had long put behind her: but for Elizabeth the Queen there could always remain the exciting pleasure of stimulating competition between men as able with tongue or pen as Sidney, Raleigh and Leicester to tell Elizabeth the woman how wonderful and beautiful she was. She chose her favourites, in the first place, not for their power to pay pretty compliments but for their possible usefulness. In respect to Essex she may have been wrong, but he had claims on her favour quite apart from his personality. His father had done her good service in Ireland and died there. His mother, her distant cousin, daughter of one of her oldest servants, Sir Francis Knollys, later married the Earl of Leicester, than whom the young Robert could have had no better sponsor at Court. He himself presently married the daughter of Sir Francis Walsingham, Sir Philip Sidney's widow. Elizabeth would have been bound to take note of so well-connected a member of her aristocracy even if he had not in himself been so singularly attractive.

His great weakness was that he could not bear her to take notice of anybody else. Almost at his first introduction to Court, after a brief spell of fighting in the Netherlands, he lost his temper because Elizabeth in some matter listened to Raleigh, an older and more experienced man, rather than to him. With any one else Elizabeth would have lost her temper, too; rather than have her do so any one else would have apologised first; but Essex mounted his high horse and would have run off to the Netherlands for some more fighting had not Elizabeth caught him in time, brought him back and forgiven him. The pattern was already set.

Jealous and headstrong, he could not bear rivals nor submit to authority, even hers; offence and forgiveness would follow until forgiveness was no longer possible.

On Leicester's resignation he was made Master of the Horse—a remunerative as well as highly ornamental office which his stepfather had held since Elizabeth's accession. Almost immediately he was in trouble again because of insulting and forcing a duel upon another courtier to whom Elizabeth had shown a small favour. Angrily she rebuked him: indeed she reminded him over and over in one form or another of what she long ago reminded Leicester, " There shall be but one mistress here and no master! " In his heart he did not believe it and he had ways of melting her. On her part, seeing how young he was, she clung to the hope that time would discipline him and make him useful as well as decorative. He was extravagant and she allowed him a good deal of money to keep up the state he felt to be proper to him; but it was never enough, and in 1589 he repeated his earlier offence, running away without permission and abandoning his duties to make his fortune by joining an expedition led by Drake against the coasts of Spain. Again Elizabeth tried to stop him, but this time he eluded her by persuading the commander of one of the vessels to sail ahead of the main fleet before her order for his return could arrive. The expedition, after a good start, sapped its strength—like many others of the time—in seeking quick profits instead of inflicting the greatest possible damage on the enemy. Essex slunk back with the rest, was scolded with the rest and like them in due course forgiven.

Yet, despite the fact that he had as yet done nothing to deserve it, such magic already attached to his name, such magnetism to his personality, that men came from everywhere clamouring to follow wherever he led; young men mostly, eager and romantic, reckless and dashing, hungry for fame and fortune; all brave and many highly talented, but too many of them impoverished, discontented and unruly. When Henry IV of France, in desperate need of help to hold his throne against his enemies, appealed to Elizabeth for an army, he specially asked that Essex, just because of this power to attract men, should be its commander. Elizabeth hesitated; lavishing honours and presents on Essex when he was under her eye was one thing, entrusting him with the lives of her men and the spending of her money quite another. But he begged and kept on begging, even on his knees, to be allowed to go, and finally she smothered her misgivings and let him. The result was again failure. Essex made a brave show. He visited Henry at his headquarters with the most brilliant retinue possible to imagine, and beat all-comers at a jumping contest. But the purpose for which he went, the capture of Rouen, he failed to achieve. In the end he was ordered home after rewarding his followers, to Elizabeth's intense annoyance, with knighthoods by the dozen for their services in an expedition that from her point of view had been a humiliating waste.

Then for a while he seemed to change. For his closest associates and advisers amongst his followers he took the two soberest and by far the ablest of them, the brothers Anthony and Francis Bacon, nephews on their mother's side of Lord Burghley. Their uncle had refused them the advancement which they—in particular Francis, who was inordinately ambitious as well as almost superhumanly intelligent—considered their due and so they turned to his and his son Robert's great rival. Anthony, the elder, a chronic invalid, had travelled widely, made friends in all sorts of places, and by means of his correspondents abroad was able to supply Essex with invaluable information which the Queen could get from no other source. Francis, possessor amongst other things of one of the best legal brains of the age, analysed political situations for him, counselled him on what course to take and how best to present his views. Elizabeth was impressed and delighted; it looked as if her problem-child was going to realise her hopes of him. Soon she felt able to fulfil one more of his desires and raise him to the Privy Council along with the Cecils, Raleigh and other pillars of her state.

But he could not keep it up. Politics were not really his line. They required patience, caution, discretion, often—when the wishes of his friends clashed with general policy—ingratitude: the colder virtues which he had been born without. Above all he lacked judgment. Taking it into his head that the Queen's physician, a Portuguese Jew named Lopez, was trying to poison her, he did not rest until he had hounded the man to the gallows. Most of those familiar with the facts thought then, and think now, that it was all a horrible mistake; and Essex, though completely sincere in what he had done, had the uncomfortable suspicion that as a result the wiser sort were secretly laughing at him. The Council table, with its long hours of close debate, was uncongenial to him; he preferred action, furious and glorious. He also yearned to give his followers what they desired, and he had no means of doing so except with the Queen's consent and at her charge. This led to endless trouble. When the office of Attorney-General fell vacant, he promised it to Francis Bacon, only to find that Elizabeth would not agree. He stormed and pleaded to no avail; Bacon was in her bad books for a speech he had made in Parliament against a grant of money;

finally she gave the office to an older and more distinguished lawyer, Sir Edward Coke, to Essex's vexation and distress. He tried to make it up to Bacon with a gift of some of his own lands, and presently with the lesser office of Solicitor-General; but again Elizabeth refused him and after some delay awarded the post to another.

Almost beside himself with frustration, Essex begged her to give him command of a great expedition forming for a raid on Cadiz, where another Armada was reported to be preparing. To this, after some hesitation, she agreed, though joining with him as Admiral the veteran Lord Howard, with Raleigh as their Rear-Admiral. The venture was a magnificent success. The fleet left Plymouth on June 3rd, 1596, and on June 21st sailed into Cadiz Harbour under the guns of the shore batteries and the ships there collected, attacking without fear, burning, destroying, forcing the Spanish captains to run their priceless galleons aground to avoid capture. Raleigh had led the actual attack on the inner harbour, but with the cordial approval of Essex, who flung his plumed hat into the harbour with an exultant shout when the decision was reached to force the defences. He returned the idol of the nation, not alone because of the victory but because of his chivalrous forbearance towards the inhabitants of the captured town. Elizabeth's pleasure, however,

was somewhat diminished when it was found that
the spoils, which properly belonged to the Treasury,
had been largely looted by the sailors. But this
negligence in no way diminished Essex's reputation
with the public; nor was it injured when he went
out again the following year in supreme command
of an expedition to the Azores for the purpose of
waylaying the Spanish treasure fleet and made a
mess of it.

His popularity was now so great that it led
directly and swiftly to his ruin. Ireland was, as
usual, in revolt, the current outbreak being of a
particularly serious nature. Previous Deputies had
failed; some one of outstanding prestige and ability
had to be sent; but few were willing to undertake
a task that had become known as the graveyard of
reputations. In the discussion over the appointment
Essex so completely lost his temper as to turn his
back on the Queen with a muttered oath. Elizabeth
responded to this unheard-of rudeness by boxing his
ears with an even stronger oath. Friends hastily
intervened, Essex fell so gravely ill as to arouse
Elizabeth's pity and alarm, and a charming apology
from him caused the quarrel to be patched up. In
the end, his pride, unwilling to disappoint the
popular belief that he was the only possible man
for the task which had proved beyond other men,
drove him to put in for the appointment himself

and after long argument he prevailed upon Elizabeth to give it to him.

So he went, with the largest army and the widest powers ever entrusted to an English commander in Ireland. His failure was proportionately complete and ignominious. Misinformed and ill-advised, nearly always in the wrong place at the wrong time, he allowed the enemy to elude and out-manœuvre him, and finally agreed to a meeting at a river-ford for the purpose of arranging an armistice. He knew that it was shameful and wrong, not at all the purpose for which the Queen had placed her resources and her good name in his hands. Worry about his ill-success, about what his rivals were saying, above all what Elizabeth was thinking of him, dogged him throughout the campaign. Of Elizabeth's opinion he could have no doubt whatever. She made it clear in her biting letters and comments, the latter only too faithfully reported to him. Made ill by his fears, he felt he could bear it no longer, and without permission left his post and hurried to London, where he hoped by his presence to undo the effects of his failure.

Weary and travel-stained, he strode unannounced into Elizabeth's presence. She greeted him kindly, as if all her old affection had been touched by seeing her prodigal return depressed and miserable after his long absence. But she had no intention of overlooking his neglect of duty. After thinking the matter over she put him under arrest with one of the Privy Council; only the strong objections of her closest advisers, who feared his popularity, dissuaded her from having his discharge of his office—and other, more sinister and secret doings there was reason to suspect—investigated by a court. Having thus spared him, she allowed her displeasure to be further softened by his increasing illness and sent her doctors to look after him, as well as many messages of inquiry and concern; presently she allowed him to return, though still nominally under arrest, to his own house.

But though pretending to feel—and perhaps feeling—gratitude, he was not at all reconciled to his situation. Power, the sense of wielding it to raise his friends and crush his enemies, was as essential to his being as submission and insignificance were hateful to it. His friends abetted him, more enthusiastically than wisely. Evidence came into the government's hands of a plot to deliver him by force, using his former troops in Ireland for the purpose: even worse, of a plot against Elizabeth herself to the benefit of one of her potential successors, James VI of Scotland, Mary Stuart's son. Elizabeth's attitude hardened; his pleas, as loving and eloquent as ever, to be admitted into her presence she rejected with harsh and sceptical words. Finally, when the evidence of grave plots brewing grew too strong to be overlooked any longer, she ordered him to account for himself before the Council.

It was the same message that had been sent to the Duke of Norfolk and other suspected persons in high place. The possible answers to it were submission, rebellion or flight. Essex was not one for submission or flight. Within the walls of Essex House in the Strand he and his hot-headed friends decided on a rebellion so woolly in intention and so confused in execution that it is impossible to this day to say precisely what they were about. Essex led a band of armed men into the City of London, whose idol he had so long been, in the hope of rallying the citizens to him with the cry that he needed their help to defend the Queen against traitors who were seeking his life. But the Council had already spread the report that it was he, in fact, who was the traitor, and the citizens turned from him as they had once turned from Wyatt. There was nothing for it but to return to Essex House and face a demand for surrender from the authorities—under the threat, said to come from the Queen herself, of blowing it up with gunpowder if he refused.

He was brought to trial before his peers and by his proud and fearless demeanour, coupled with his unconcealed contempt for his enemies present, added the last great scene to the drama of the reign.

Sentenced to death, he made no move to save himself by an appeal to the Queen, though during the period of his disgrace he had made many of the sort she had never hitherto been able to resist. It would perhaps in any event have been useless; her mind was made up, and whatever the agony she felt on confirming the sentence, outwardly she showed almost none; she hesitated far more over the deaths of Mary Stuart and Norfolk, whom she had loved far less. Perhaps it was for that very reason, that the love she had given him he had not scrupled to betray. Had he loved her in return as he should have done, he would have respected the strength of her mind as well as trying to exploit the weakness of her heart and not failed to recognise the great Queen in the ageing and loving woman. For that mistake he paid the penalty on Tower Hill in February, 1601, accepting his fate gallantly while at last humbly admitting his fault to the sovereign who had so greatly honoured and so patiently borne with him.

Elizabeth survived him two years. In some ways they were the saddest of her life, for they were lonely and she dreaded the end that she knew could not be far off. She was still as vigorous as ever, as active in the affairs of state, more popular, if anything, and admired at home and abroad. But her power of love seems to have been spent with Essex, and the others, the friends of her own generation whom she had most cared for and trusted, were swiftly disappearing. Lord Burghley went in 1598, her closest woman friend and oldest after Katherine Ashley, who died a few years earlier, the Countess of Nottingham in 1602. Even her oldest enemy, once her suitor and brother-in-law, Philip II of Spain, was gone after a long and painful illness, leaving her the oldest reigning monarch in Europe. More and more she looked upon herself as the matriarch, the mother of her people; the fact comes out increasingly in her public speeches; the image of herself she had created and encouraged, as wife to England and mistress to an adoring circle of men, had already begun to fade into legend. She knew, and the knowledge was perhaps the most poignant part of her sadness, that with the awe and veneration in which her subjects held her was mixed a certain expectation, eager as well as apprehensive, of who, and what, would come after her. It was no secret to her, though she gave no sign, that even those closest to her were making their own arrangements with her possible successors . . . Cecil and his group with James of Scotland (with whom Essex, too, had been in furtive correspondence)—Raleigh with another Stuart whom he and his friends preferred.

But even this was one of her triumphs, her last

and, so far as England's peace was concerned, amongst her greatest. For none dared do more than make ready and wait; the long-standing danger of a violent upheaval at her death had almost vanished, because she had allowed no pretender to build up a following or to assert any claim on her subjects' loyalty which could remotely compare with her own. And this was because to the very end she remained herself, what she had always been—at once imperious and approachable, confident and watchful, shrewdly understanding of human beings and their motives yet at her delighted and delightful best in their company; never for a moment doubting that her people's welfare and her own were one and the same because God had arranged it so. She herself wrote her own, and perhaps the best, epitaph on her reign when she said in her last great speech from the throne:

"And though God hath raised me high, yet this I account the glory of my crown, that I have reigned with your loves. This makes me that I do not so much rejoice that God hath made me to be a Queen, as to be a Queen over so thankful a people, and to be the means under God to conserve you in safety and to preserve you from danger . . ."

So it came about that the most of her subjects,

sharing this belief in her divine appointment, allowed her to make the supreme decision for which they had so long waited in her own time and way. She designated no one by name, even after she fell seriously ill owing to wilful exposure to the early March winds in her seventieth year, for to have done so might have started the trouble she had all her reign been at pains to avoid. But she allowed Cecil and his associates, now by her own will and consent the dominant party in her councils, quietly to give assurances to James VI, the natural heir by blood and ancient constitutional practice and therefore by far the most acceptable to the nation as a whole. As she sat shivering with fever—for she would not allow her doctors to order her to bed—the machinery was set in motion, the proclamation drawn, which would make Mary Stuart's son James I of England: and on March 24th, 1603, he succeeded to the throne as peacefully as she vacated it in the early hours of that morning.